Story-Shaped Christology
The Role of Narratives in
Identifying Jesus Christ

Theological Inquiries

Studies in Contemporary
Biblical and Theological Problems

PAULIST PRESS
New York ● Mahwah

Story-Shaped Christology

The Role of Narratives in Identifying Jesus Christ

Robert A. Krieg, C.S.C.

PAULIST PRESS
New York • Mahwah

In gratitude
to my
father and mother

Library of Congress Cataloging-in-Publication Data

Krieg, Robert A., 1946–
    Story-shaped Christology.

    (Theological inquiries)
    Includes bibliographies.
    1. Jesus Christ—Person and offices.   2. Story-
telling (Christian theology)   I. Title.   II. Series.
BT202.K73   1988   232   87-25904
ISBN 0-8091-2941-8 (pbk.)

Published by Paulist Press
997 Macarthur Boulevard
Mahwah, N.J. 07430

Printed and bound in the United States of America

CONTENTS

PREFACE

Many people have made this book possible, and some of them can be named here in gratitude.

Paulist Press' editors, Lawrence Boadt and Robert Hamma, along with its readers, have offered sound advice.

The University of Notre Dame is a community of faith and learning conducive to theology. Undergraduate and graduate students have criticized and refined this book's ideas. I have received assistance from the faculty and staff of the Department of Theology, especially Richard McBrien. Roberta Ferkins has ably assisted with my administrative tasks, and Suzanne Fournier has brought her editing skills to these pages. Parts of this text have been critically read by colleagues: Harold Attridge, David Burrell, James Burtchaell, Regina Coll, Stanley Hauerwas, Catherine Mowry LaCugna, Thomas O'Meara, Mark Searle and David Stosur. Mr. and Mrs. Arthur J. Decio have generously given the College of Arts and Letters a research home.

Prof. Dr. Walter Kasper (Tübingen) and Dr. Josef Meyer zu Schlochtern (Bochum) have patiently explained aspects of German theology.

Many years ago, I was introduced to Christology by Robert Kruse, Stonehill College (North Easton, MA), and I was encouraged by William Ribando to pursue this interest while teaching at King's College (Wilkes-Barre, PA).

I am deeply grateful to friends, the Holy Cross community, and my family.

Easter 1987

Chapter One

WHO IS JESUS CHRIST TODAY?

On Sunday, September 29, 1963, Pope Paul VI opened the second session of the Second Vatican Council with an historic address. After praising his predecessor, the new Pontiff took up John XXIII's call for renewal. He charged the Council to give a fresh view of the Church, to promote Christian unity, and to engage in dialogue with the contemporary world. Paul VI linked these tasks with faithfulness to Jesus Christ: "[H]ere and at this very hour we should proclaim Christ to ourselves and to the world around us; Christ our beginning, Christ our life and our guide, Christ our hope and our end."[1] When, after an hour, the Bishop of Rome ended what he termed his "first encyclical," all assembled in St. Peter's Basilica knew that there would be no turning back. Paul VI had secured John XXIII's "*aggiornamento.*"

Sixteen years later another newly elected Pontiff issued his first formal statement. On March 4, 1979, in his encyclical *Redemptor Hominis,* John Paul II committed himself to renewing the Church. As Paul VI (d. 1978) had done, the former archbishop of Krakow called for the Church's reform, binding it to Jesus Christ. John Paul II accentuated the mystery of the Church's founder: "Our spirit is set in one direction, the only direction for our intellect, will and heart—toward Christ our Redeemer, toward Christ, the Redeemer of man."[2] Further: "The Church's fundamental function in every age and particularly in ours is . . . to help all men to be familiar with the profundity of the redemption taking place in Christ Jesus."[3] What was one theme among others in Paul VI's address became the major thrust of John Paul's: For authentic renewal, the Church must live in union with Christ.

Paul VI's and John Paul II's statements show a shift in emphasis. From Vatican Council I through Vatican Council II Church leaders grappled with ecclesiology. Paul VI and the Council treated the nature of the

3

Church, the authority of the bishops, and the Church's mission in the modern world. Since Vatican II these issues persist, but they are seen in relation to Christology. In his first encyclical John Paul II has given priority to Christ's redeeming activity in the world within which the Church is "the community of disciples."[4] This view represents what many Christians now see. We have become increasingly aware that our identity depends upon the identity of the one to whom we dedicate our lives. "If Vatican III were to meet [now]," observed Gerald O'Collins in 1977, "its major document would not be 'The Church in the Modern World' but some response to the question: Who is Jesus Christ for us today?"[5]

This emphasis on Jesus Christ is also found in the work of many contemporary theologians.[6] In the past two decades there have appeared significant Christological texts by Frans Jozef van Beeck, Leonardo Boff, Eugene Borowitz, John Cobb, Hans Frei, Rosemary Haughton, Monica Hellwig, Peter C. Hodgson, Walter Kasper, Hans Küng, Gerald O'Collins, Schubert Ogden, Wolfhart Pannenberg, Karl Rahner (d. 1984), Edward Schillebeeckx, Piet Schoonenberg, Juan Luis Segundo, Jon Sobrino, William M. Thompson, and Patricia Wilson-Kastner. What is striking about a list like this is that many more names could be added to it. Numerous theologians are participating in the Church's effort to identify its Founder. I too want to support this endeavor.

In this chapter and the ones to follow I shall clarify the process by which we answer "Who is Jesus Christ today?"[7] My thesis is that the explicit use of narratives can strengthen Christology. Just as we often say who someone is by telling his or her life story, so too our research into the identity of Jesus Christ can employ different forms of narratives, namely, historical reconstructions about Jesus, the Gospels as stories, and the lives of the saints. This is not to say that Christology should be reduced to storytelling. On the contrary. Narratives can provide a systematic inquiry with specific ways to structure its Christology.

This call for narrative theology is not new. Others have already made it. Since 1972, in numerous essays, Johann Baptist Metz has envisioned a "post-idealistic theology," relying on narratives.[8] In *Blessed Rage for Order* (1975) David Tracy has acknowledged the place of story in Christology.[9] Hans Frei has demonstrated how Christology can depend on "the Gospel story" in *The Identity of Jesus Christ* (1975).[10] In *Models of Revelation* (1983) Avery Dulles has included the category narrative among the kinds of "symbolic mediation" of God's revelation.[11] Along with these texts there are a number of careful studies on theology and narrative. These include George Stroup's *The Promise of Narrative Theology* (1981), John Navone's and Thomas Cooper's *Tellers of the Word* (1981), Michael Goldberg's *Theology and Narrative* (1982), Terrence Tilley's *Story Theology* (1985) and Ronald Thiemann's *Revelation and Theology* (1986).[12] This short list names but a few titles from a lengthy one of books and articles, some of which I will cite as we proceed.

What is new in this study? Rather than lay out a theory to support theologians' use of narratives, this book highlights the ways three recent Christologies actually depend on narratives in order to identify Jesus Christ. In *Jesus the Christ* Kasper has demonstrated that Christology can draw on three sources: historical research into Jesus' life and times, Christian testimony to the risen Christ, and the experience of the contemporary Church.[13] Crucial to these sources are their narratives. Further, Schillebeeckx in *Jesus* has constructed an historical narrative about Jesus and proposed that it can generate a new Christology.[14] Moreover, in *Christ Proclaimed* van Beeck has recounted the story told by Matthew, Mark and Luke, and from this he has presented Jesus Christ as the perfect relation between God and creation.[15] To be sure, these three Christologies exhibit distinct methods and views of Jesus Christ. Yet, they stand together in their reliance on narratives, and therefore they convey some of the ways that narratives can shape Christology.

One part of the following book is analysis. Chapters Two, Three and Four study *Jesus the Christ, Jesus* and *Christ Proclaimed*. The other part of this book is more constructive. Chapter Five builds on the Christologies of Kasper, Schillebeeckx and van Beeck. It presents a story-shaped Christology, in which a retelling of Mark's Gospel, an historical narrative of Jesus' ministry, and a biography of Dorothy Day are the sources for identifying Jesus Christ as the founder of the new people of compassion. The logic of this inquiry is then discussed in Chapter Six with help from works by Alasdair MacIntyre and Paul Ricoeur.

Talk about Jesus Christ can become tangled, for it can be distracted by the fact that he is a special case. Christ does indeed bear a singular relation to God and to the human community, but this does not mean that talk about him is so unusual that it does not resemble ordinary discourse.[16] The language of Christology is similar to our usual attempts to say who someone is. Theologians depend on analogy, and in their respective works Kasper, Schillebeeckx and van Beeck have done just this. They have been guided by our familiar logic of personal identification. What is this logic, and how does it influence Christology? I shall pursue this question in this first chapter's two major sections. Section one reviews our familiar process of identifying another person, and section two considers how we can give an individuating account of Jesus Christ. This first chapter will equip us to study how different kinds of narratives can function in a systematic response to "Who is Jesus Christ today?"

I.1 *Identifying Another Person*

When we are asked "Who is that person?" we usually mention a name and then give a title, e.g., "Doctor." Sometimes this is enough. But at other times more is needed. If so, we tell anecdotes. For example: "She is the woman who last year won the Merit Award." To identify someone we recount some of the things the person has done and endured. If more still needs to be known, then we review the person's life, during at least a limited period of time. In other words, we resort to biography. This way of identifying a person exhibits a pattern which requires further comment.[17]

"Who is so-and-so?" directs attention to the person as person. To see this, contrast it with "What is so-and-so?" What-questions classify persons in terms of functions and types. In response to "What is she?" we might say, for instance, "She is a physician." This expresses her professional role. In response to "What kind of person is she?" we might say "She has an extrovert personality" or "She is an honest person." These answers place the individual within categories to which other men and women belong. This is not the case with the who-question. It views persons in relation to their lives, for anecdotes and biography focus on persons within their respective histories. Therefore, whereas what-questions view persons in relation to functions and types, the who-question regards the character of the persons themselves.

The personal direction of the who-question prompts us to respond to it by giving names and titles.[18] A name is person-directed, for it serves as a tag. It singles out people by pointing to them. Titles refer to people in a more complicated way. On the one hand, titles take their meaning from the social structure within which they function. For example, to say that someone is president of the United States is to locate the person within an institution. In this perspective, titles are not person-directed. But on the other hand, titles often receive their specific meaning from the conduct of the person to whom they are ascribed. For example, both Jimmy Carter and Ronald Reagan have served as U.S. president, and the title ''president'' means something quite different when applied to each man. To some extent, the meaning of a title is governed by the person who bears it, and therefore there is a sense in which titles like names are person-directed. We know what the title means by knowing the individual to whom it points.

This brings us to a limit of names and titles in answering ''Who is so-and-so?'' Names and, to some extent, titles point to their reference. They function best when we already know about the person to whom they refer, and then we can link the name or title with the individual. What do we do however when this external connection cannot occur? This is when we adopt forms of description.

One form of description is an account of the person's physical features. We describe the person's age, height, weight, hair, complexion, posture and mannerisms. Frequently this allows us to single the person out in a crowd. Such a response to the who-question has the advantage of not merely pointing, as names do, but it is inadequate in that two or more people may resemble each other. Moreover, physical description does not reach deeply enough into personal existence. It presents persons as objects, neglecting their personalities, experiences and life goals. Physical description does not therefore suffice when answering ''Who is so-and-so?''

Another form of description by which we identify someone is the category narrative. Our attempts to provide an individuating account usually include anecdotes and biographies. We focus on the person by recalling the person's words, deeds and life. Hannah Arendt makes this point when she writes: ''*Who* somebody is or was we can know only by knowing the story of which he is himself the hero—his biography, in other words; everything else we know of him, including the work he may have produced and left behind, tells us only *what* he is or was.''[19]

Why is this? Why do we identify persons by telling their life stories? In part, it has to do with the nature of personal existence, and to this I shall turn shortly. Further, in part our reliance on anecdotes and biographies stems from the nature of this kind of description. A good anecdote or biography hangs together. It coheres so that it creates a world in which persons interact with one another and their situation.[20] Who someone is is a function of what the person says, does and endures in this world. Thus, an anecdote or biography gives a context in which we can place a person and identify him or her. Moreover, this context is not a set of classifications but a series of events, a drama. Thus, we see the person in action over a course of time, and we see the person's line of continuity, that which remains the same. Anecdotes and biographies can be aesthetic units which create a world inhabited by the person whom we want to know, and they describe this person as he or she acts, suffers and persists over a period of time. In sum, these narratives are person-directed, and therefore they can provide answers to the who-question which is also directed to persons as persons.

Talk about biography raises of course many issues.[21] More than one biography can be written about a life. Much depends upon the life itself, the author of the biography, and the relationship between the author and the subject. But we need not pursue all of this here. My point is simply this. We often find that full answers to "Who is so-and-so?" include anecdotes and biographies. Identifying someone appears therefore to depend upon the use of different kinds of narratives as well as on names, titles and physical description.

Finally, we rely on yet another form of discourse. This is conceptual discourse, language characterized more by the use of ideas than by images, and thus possessing a high degree of generality without the loss of clarity.[22] The question about one person's identity can lead to a comparison between this life and others, and also to a discussion of personal existence in general. Once we know someone's life story we can find ourselves asking "How is this person unique?" That is: "How does this person's life and configuration of personal qualities distinguish him or her from other men and women?" Moreover, we might query "What is the truth of this life?" and "What does this one life reveal about personal existence in general?" Once we pursue questions like these, we adopt a language that permits us to talk about personal existence in general. This language employs concepts of person so that an individual can be seen in relation to the idea of being a person.

Often we say who someone is or was without being aware that we are following a pattern which unfolds with distinct components. The who-question leads from names and titles to physical description, and physical description moves to anecdotes and biographies. Further, biographies can answer the question of personal identity, but they also lead beyond the study of one human being to a consideration of personal existence in general. To put this another way, our use of narratives can bring us to conceptual or thematic discourse. It does this because ideas of personal identity and personal existence are implicit in the process of saying who someone is. To these I will now turn.

I.2 *Personal Identity*

"Personal identity" is a complex notion. It refers to that which remains the same in a person throughout a life. A synonym for "personal identity" is "personal continuity." Both phrases express that particular dynamism which is denoted by the indexical term "I." Frei describes "personal identity" by using the metaphor of a "core." He writes: "Loosely speaking, the word ['personal identity'] indicates the very 'core' of a person toward which everything else is ordered, like spokes to the center of a wheel."[23] While this account is helpful in highlighting the persistent element in personal existence, it risks reducing this to a single point.[24] To fill out this understanding let us consider that a person consists of the three dimensions of length, breadth and depth.

First, persons have histories. Persons take shape as they abide and interact in the world. In his philosophical discussion of personal identity, Sydney Shoemaker observes that personal identity entails "persistence in time."[25] The "I" is formed in the course of time as one intends, acts and suffers within a natural and social environment. In this same vein, Schillebeeckx observes that the "I" includes "the past events that have surrounded him" and also "the effect he has had on subsequent history."[26] Personal identity is arrived at and manifest in one's length of days. Richard Taylor asserts this when he states that:

> . . . a person undergoes constant change and renewal over the course of time, such that he is in some respects the same today as he was yesterday and in some respects different, that over the course of sufficient time, he undergoes a total renewal such that he shares no cell or particle with a former self long since

past, but that he is nevertheless *the same person* in this relative sense, that he *grew out of* that former person.[27]

Persons exist as physical beings. They are flesh and blood. To be sure, they change physically—especially today in light of medical advances. Yet, persons are in part a function of physical, genetic and racial factors. Richard Taylor writes: "The connection between yourself and your body is far more intimate and metaphysical than anything else you can think of. One's body is at least a part of himself, and is so regarded by everyone."[28] Bernard Williams corroborates this view when he insists that personal existence, as we know it, entails embodiment.[29]

Second, persons are constituted by their relationships with the world, especially with other people. Persons may be influenced by their interaction with events, physical reality and society. In particular, the "I" is defined by the "we," by a person's bonds with other men and women. Schillebeeckx, for instance, notes that no one can be understood "independently of his relations with those about him, contemporaries who have received from him and in turn have influenced him and touched off specific reactions in him."[30] Therefore, when we wish to know someone, we may need to know those with whom the person associates.

Third, persons are more than their histories and their associations. They are also determined by their point of view on their histories and relationships. A person's self-consciousness shapes in part who the person is, as John Locke (d. 1704) and philosophical discussions since Locke have stressed.[31] Personal existence depends upon memory. The recollection of events and persons binds these together in relation to our lives. One's history and involvements with other men and women are united in part because one remembers them.[32] Moreover, self-consciousness involves taking a stance in relation to what one remembers and is currently involved in. A person possesses an outlook or perspective from which one recollects the past and faces the world. In sum, memory and viewpoint provide persons with a mode of interpreting their lives, and this interpretation is part of their identity. George Stroup makes this point when he states: "A person's identity, therefore, is an interpretation of personal history in which the meaning of the whole and hence the identity of the self is constructed on the foundation of a few basic events and the symbols and concepts used to interpret them."[33]

Personal identity is, as Frei states, that which remains the same in a person. Yet, this "core" is three dimensional. It consists of the length of one's history, the breadth of one's involvements, and the depth of one's self-reflection. To put this succinctly, personal identity is one's continuity. This continuity consists however not of a single line, but of a convergence of lines. A person's persistence in human affairs, bonds with others, and memory and outlook on life define that person. This is the mysterious reality to which we point when we name a person. Stephen Crites expresses this well when he writes:

> Our sense of personal identity depends upon the continuity of experience through time, a continuity bridging even the cleft between remembered past and projected future. Given when it is largely implicit, not vividly self-conscious, our sense of ourselves is at every moment to some extent integrated into a single story.[34]

Finally, this understanding of personal identity allows us to appreciate the appropriateness of biography for personal identification. Biography, a form of the category narrative, is capable of expressing a person's length, breadth and depth. Biography encompasses the unfolding of events, the interaction of agents, the relating of men and women, and their self-reflections. Because of this, biography not only points to a person, it may also represent the person by conveying the dimensions of this life. Biography can manifest the continuity of a life, and hence it can reveal a person. That reality to which names and titles refer and which discursive language locates in general classifications can also be expressed in narrative.

I.3 *Notions of Person*

Three concepts of person correspond to the three aspects of personal identity. These are: person as agent, person as relation, and person as subject.[35] Person as agent conceives of a person in his or her action. It highlights the unfolding or length of a life. Person as relation conceives of a person in community. It accentuates the web of relationships or breadth of a life. Person as subject views a person in terms of self-consciousness. It illuminates the subjectivity or depth of personal existence. Each of these notions requires a brief comment.

Person as agent regards action as the primary form of personal expression.[36] A person is what he or she says and does. In this view, Rene Descartes' (d. 1650) "I think, therefore I am" is made subordinate to "I do, therefore I am." Cornelius van Peursen makes this point when he observes that "the 'I' must not be conceived of primarily as a thinking or perceiving subject, but as acting and doing."[37] To be a person is to be one who initiates change, brings something about, and is responsible for this new state of affairs.

Person as agent rests on the conviction that intentions are realized in saying and doing. What I intend in my action is evident, under ordinary conditions, to other men and women who observe my conduct. Moreover, when these intentions are deep-seated, their realization in my behavior reveals me, my "self." I am not disconnected from my action; rather I am integrated in what I do, and I make myself known to others. In van Peursen's words, "the 'I' of another person is manifested in all that he does. It is not something behind or among these doings of his, but is their total cohesion—is precisely that."[38] Hannah Arendt describes it thus:

> In acting and speaking, men show who they are, reveal actively their unique personal identities and thus make their appearance in the human world, while their physical identities appear without any activity of their own in the unique shape of the body and sound of the voice.[39]

In action a person becomes an individual, for action unites a person's complex of intentions, thoughts, affections and embodiment. John Macmurray writes: "The Self, then, is not the thinker but the doer. In its positive doing it is agent; in its negative doing it is subject."[40] That is, a person becomes integrated as he or she acts, and as a result action is the primary moment of personal expression. But action without reflection loses its orientation and thus ceases to be action. Therefore, in Macmurray's view the notion of personal agency is linked to other ideas of person. Action springs from a person's relationships with others and simultaneously deepens these, and further action requires self-awareness.

Person as relation rests on the recognition that personal existence is communal. Who I am depends in part upon the men and women with whom I live and work. Martin Buber (d. 1965) grasped the centrality of the relational aspect of being a person.[41] He insisted that personal existence is not primarily a matter of I-it, of the self relating to objects. Rather, personal existence is constituted by the I-Thou, by the self relating to other selves. To be a person is therefore to be a relation. This concept of person as relation is articulated by Macmurray when he states "that the Self is constituted by its relation to the Other; that it has its being in its relationship; that this relationship is necessarily personal."[42]

Often we do not accomplish what we set out to do. Our intentions, at least as we initially hold them, are modified in our give-and-take with the world. Our actions come about as we interact with other persons, events and physical realities. Moreover, we do not fashion our intentions in isolation from other people. Other men and women influence what we hope for, think and initiate. Others call us into being and sustain us in this development. In a word, personal existence is relational. Yet, our relating to others is also connected to our relating to ourselves.

Person as subject recognizes that personal existence requires self-consciousness. To be a person is to be aware of one's intentions, feelings, thoughts and conduct. Thus, speech includes the use of the self-referential word "I." The person or self has a perspective on the world; it stands in the world and yet apart from it. Person as subject, says Ludwig Wittgenstein (d. 1951), is similar to the eye as seer, for it looks on the world but is not seen.[43] The self, like the eye, is a limit of the world.

The capability for self-reflection distinguishes persons from objects. Whereas an inanimate object (e.g., a stone) can be satisfactorily analyzed through empirical methods, for example, by weighing and chemical tests, a person is not fully known by means of scientific studies, for example, through sociological, economic and psychological profiles. A person possesses a subjectivity, a relating to self, that in part defines the person. This view is articulated by Martin Heidegger (d. 1975) when he writes: "The question of the 'who' answers itself in terms of the 'I' itself, the 'subject,' the 'Self.' The 'who' is what maintains itself as something identical throughout changes in its experiences and ways of behaviour, and which relates itself to this changing multiplicity in so doing."[44]

Person as subject is essential to our understanding of personal existence. So too are person as agent and person as relation. Being a person is such a rich reality that it can best be apprehended by more than one notion. Each of the three concepts we have reviewed captures an aspect of personal existence while also allowing for other complementary views of what it means to be a person.

Moreover, these three views of person are inherent in talk about personal identity. Person as agent is implied by our attentiveness to a person's words and deeds. A biography depends upon descriptions of what a person said and did. Person as relation is operative in biography, for we need to appreciate the circles of friends and acquaintances with whom the person interacted. It is implied as well in our recognition of the social, historical and economic factors in a person's world. Person as subject is manifest in biography when a person's self-disclosive statements are quoted. ''I''-statements allow us to apprehend a person's self-awareness. In conclusion, then, our ordinary response to ''Who is so-and-so?'' depends on at least three ideas of person: person as agent, person as relation, and person as subject.

II.1 *Identifying Jesus Christ*

Analogy goes from the known to the unknown. It extends our ordinary use of words so that we can talk about something which is similar to and yet different from the usual realities about which we speak. In the words of David Tracy, analogy is ''a language of ordered relationships articulating similarity in difference.''[45] Further, according to David Burrell, analogy ''is closely linked to a purposive use of language.''[46] We extend our use of words in order to speak about something beyond the usual reach of our discourse. Therefore, as both Tracy and Burrell remind us, analogy is one of theology's primary forms of discourse. We apply to God patterns of speech that do not properly fit God, and we qualify this talk so that it more accurately reflects the mystery of God. One such pattern of speech is the process of identifying a person. We adopt this familiar logic to answer, ''Who is Jesus Christ?''

''Who is Jesus Christ?'' is similar to and yet different from ''Who is so-and-so?'' asked of any ordinary person. It is similar in that it directs attention to Jesus' words, deeds and life. That is, the who-question does not call for locating Jesus Christ within categories, as occurs with "What does it mean to speak, as Chalcedon does, of Jesus Christ as 'truly God' and 'truly man'?" Nor does it set up a comparison between Jesus Christ and other religious leaders, as can happen with "How is Jesus Christ unique?" When applied to Jesus Christ, the who-question asks about this "person" as it asks about any person's life and involvements.

Yet, "Who is Jesus Christ?" is unlike "Who is so-and-so?" because Jesus Christ is now known in light of his resurrection. The present tense in "Who is Jesus Christ?" expresses the mystery of this life and therefore conveys an unusual meaning, whereas in the case of all other men and women we eventually shift to the past tense, "Who was so-and-so?" This need not occur in talk about Jesus Christ. Since he is a living reality, he is contemporaneous with every age. This means that the question about the identity of Jesus Christ demands an answer whose logic is not exactly like the one that we ordinarily follow in response to the who-question. The language of identifying Jesus Christ is therefore not the same as but analogous to the pattern we reviewed in the first section of this chapter. We can see this as we consider Christology's use of names, titles, and historical reconstruction.

A person stands at the center of Christian belief. He is called "Jesus Christ" which consists of both a name, "Jesus," and a title, "Christ." "Jesus Christ" is therefore more than a tag. Not only does it refer to this individual, it also makes a claim about him. "Jesus Christ" declares something—this person is a special case, for knowing him entails more than knowing Jesus of Nazareth. "Jesus of Nazareth" is the name of a past figure whom we must indeed seek to know if we are to understand Jesus Christ. But knowledge of the historical person does not suffice for apprehending the present and future reality, Jesus Christ.

Along with the title "Christ," this person receives other titles (for example, "Son of God" and "Lord") and here too we are reminded that we speak in analogy. On the one hand, these titles are ascribed to Jesus Christ in a way similar to our ascription of titles to other men and women.[47] Thus part of what they mean is determined by convention. "Son of God" and "Lord" functioned in the life of Israel apart from Jesus, and therefore this history determines in part what they mean when they are applied to Jesus. On the other hand, the meaning of "Son of God" and "Lord" also depends in part on how they are redefined by their recipient. To an extent, this is common, for a person's conduct influences the meaning of his or her titles. But the case of Jesus exhibits a special feature.

As the Christian community has increased its understanding of the person to whom it is dedicated, the titles have functioned in new ways, thereby changing their meaning. The Church has come to realize that there is a quantum leap between these titles' shades of meaning when applied to other figures and the meaning of these same titles when ascribed to Jesus. For example, it may be said of another religious leader that this person is *a* son or daughter of God, but Christians speak of Jesus as *the* "Son of God." For Christians this person exists in a singular relationship with God, and therefore he gives a radically new significance to whatever titles he receives.

As we saw in the first section, our identification of another person relies not only on names and titles but also on physical description. In the case of Jesus Christ such a depiction is in fact impossible, since we simply lack the sources for this. Further, if it were possible, the theological import of a physical description would be two-sided. First, we must recognize Jesus' corporeality, for he was flesh and blood as all of us are. Moreover, his resurrection included his whole person. Second, a physical description of Jesus of Nazareth is not a prerequisite to identifying him. What is crucial, however, is his character as disclosed in his actions and life. Thus, for the purposes of identification, it suffices to know the minimum, for example, that he was a Palestinian Jew from Galilee who lived in the second temple period.

We usually turn to biography when a name, titles and physical description do not say all that we need to say about a person, and, given the mysterious complexity of Jesus Christ, we do require something more than titles and a vague physical sketch if we are to know him. A fuller, more descriptive account is needed in order to clarify the reality to which the name and titles refer. To an extent, this is no different from our attempts to identify any person. We often resort to anecdotes and biographies to say all that must be said. But, when discussing Jesus Christ, we encounter two difficulties. First, biographies of Jesus are in fact not possible, for the historical data is lacking. Second, even if a biography of Jesus could be written, this would be insufficient for our knowledge of him. With these two points, we have reached the terrain crossed by recent "quests" for the historical Jesus. Let us therefore take each in turn.

First, what can we say about the life of Jesus of Nazareth? Since we do not have the historical data, we cannot write a biography of Jesus.[48] Nor can we give even a chronicle of events in his life. Yet, we can form an historical reconstruction of some aspects of Jesus' life and times. In recent years historians and biblical exegetes have reached a general consensus about key features of Jesus' words, deeds and life, and on the basis of this we can fashion an historical narrative, not unlike a rough biographical sketch, about Jesus' ministry and death. An example of this is given by Schillebeeckx who in *Jesus* describes this account as "a post-critical narrative history."[49] In light of Schillebeeckx's work, we see that while we cannot provide a detailed response to "Who was Jesus of Nazareth?" we can provide a loose historical narrative about Jesus of Nazareth.

Second, what is the theological import of this historical narrative? Those who undertook the late nineteenth century's original quest for the historical Jesus offer one answer. According to such writers as Ernst Renan (d. 1892), Adolf von Harnack (d. 1930) and Shailer Matthews (d. 1941) the object of faith is Jesus of Nazareth, and therefore an historical narrative about Jesus might undergird Christian claims. In their respective works each of these scholars tried to tell a biography that would stand as the basis of Christian belief. Norman Perrin (d. 1976) has succinctly described the "liberal" quest's aim:

> This epitomizes the concern of liberal scholarship, namely, to establish by historical-critical methodology the authentic teaching of Jesus and the historical core of the gospel narratives concerning his life, to recapture the person mirrored in that teaching and revealed in that life, to accept that person and that teaching as the concern and object of faith, and to seek to imitate and to learn from him.[50]

This view was overturned, in the first part of the twentieth century, by such scholars as Martin Kähler (d. 1912), Albert Schweitzer (d. 1965), Karl Barth (d. 1968) and Rudolf Bultmann (d. 1976). These theologians took issue with the liberal quest's assumption that faith rests on the historical Jesus. Christian belief, they argued, does not primarily concern an historical person but the risen Christ. Belief begins in response to Jesus' resurrection. These theologians remind us, as Perrin states, that: "The object of Christian faith is the historic Christ, the Christ of the kerygma, and not the historical Jesus."[51] What then, according to this view, is the theological significance of history? In general, it simply assures us, insists the "dialectical theologians," that Jesus lived, preached and died on a cross.

This second answer to the question of history's significance for belief and theology has been followed by a third. In 1953 Ernst Käsemann, a student of Bultmann, initiated the "new quest" with his lecture "The Problem of the Historical Jesus."[52] Käsemann persuasively argued that the first Christian preaching, as found for example in 1 Corinthians 15:3–5, includes historical data, and it does so because what Jesus' followers proclaimed about him after his resurrection is based in part upon features of his life prior to his death. Through the work of such theologians as Käsemann, Gunther Bornkamm and Hans Conzelmann the new quest has established a position between the extremes of the liberal quest and dialectical theology. On the one hand, it acknowledges that Christian faith is directed toward the risen Christ. On the other, it recognizes the importance of what Perrin calls a "material continuity" between the historical Jesus and the Christ of faith.[53] History contributes to our understanding of the risen Christ because it highlights the historical Jesus' trust in God as Abba and therefore implies his bond with God.

We have a common way of answering "Who is so-and-so?": We give a name, titles, physical description and a biography. When we ask however "Who is Jesus Christ?" we can follow the usual form of response only to a limited degree. "Jesus Christ" consists of a name and a title, and all titles when applied to this person take on a new meaning. Physical description is not only impossible, it is also secondary to knowing the "person" who lives today in God's Spirit. Finally, a biography is not possible, and while a loose biographical sketch may be possible, it cannot express fully the reality of the risen Lord. What a historical narrative can achieve, though, is important. As the new questers have argued, it can focus on Jesus of Nazareth so that light is shed on the character of the risen Lord. For instance, it can provide a glimpse of Jesus' sense of intimacy with God, thereby pointing toward his full identity. This leads however to a central question: What do we mean when we talk about the identity of Jesus Christ?

II.2 *The Identity of Jesus Christ*

Personal identity is a complex idea, and it becomes even more intricate when applied to Jesus Christ. In ordinary usage personal identity depends on the unfolding of one's life, web of relationships and self-understanding, and therefore it consists of a person's continuity. But how does this apply to Jesus Christ? When Christians speak of his "life," they have in mind a reality that extends beyond death. When they consider his relationships, they talk not only about his bonds with Peter, James and John who knew Jesus prior to his death, but also about his encounter with Paul. Also, when Christians reflect on Jesus' sense of self, they think of Christ's union with God in the Spirit. How then can we talk about the identity of Jesus Christ in a way that on the one hand respects this mystery and on the other takes its bearings from our familiar patterns of discourse?

We can speak about the identity of Jesus Christ, I propose, by relying on three different kinds of narratives. Whereas we can ordinarily grasp who someone is by telling a biography, in the case of Jesus Christ we need not only a rough biographical sketch, but also something more. We need narratives that allow us to convey the continuity of this life beyond death. Two such kinds of narratives are the Gospels and biographies of exemplary Christians. Through the use of historical narratives about Jesus, the Gospels as stories, and critical recollections of the saints' lives, we are able to perceive Christ from three perspectives.

First, an historical narrative about Jesus can partially reveal Christ. In this perspective, the continuity of this life runs from birth to death, as it does for any human being. Jesus gains his identity in the course of his life, ministry and last days, as he interacts with his disciples, the people and the authorities. Moreover, this history and interaction influence his self-understanding which in turn shapes his future and his involvements. This outlook is manifest, for example, in his sayings and parables. When we assemble historical data about Jesus' life, involvements and outlook, we have at hand the material for a rough biographical sketch, for an historical narrative of the sort fashioned by Schillebeeckx in *Jesus*.

A second perspective on the identity of Jesus Christ reaches beyond his death to his presence among the first Christians. In this view the length of this life does not stop with the cross but extends into the first Christian communities. The breadth of his identity encompasses the interaction between the risen Lord and the New Testament communities, for example, those of Paul and the evangelists. The depth of his life includes Jesus' special bond with God, as presented by the various scriptural testimonies. To apprehend this Jesus we rely on biblical narratives as literary units, for example, on the Gospels, since their scope is broader than that allowed by the canons of modern historical methods.

The third view of the identity of Jesus Christ searches for the risen Lord today. This is the Christ who encounters Christians at the Lord's Supper as well as in their service for the coming of God's "kingdom." In this view, the length and breadth and depth of Christ is expressed in the Church's tradition, for example, in its worship, service, teachings, and Christian lives. Moreover, this knowledge of Christ entails the study of tradition and contemporary culture. One specific way to pursue this third approach to Christ is through the lives of saints. In every age singular women and men emerge who mirror the face of Christ. By knowing the length and breadth and depth of their lives, we can indirectly identify Christ in a given era. Biographies of Christ's twentieth century disciples can afford us therefore knowledge of Christ today.

In order to have a full account of Jesus Christ's identity, we need to view his life from more than one perspective. If we were to limit ourselves to one approach to Jesus, for example, to historical reconstruction, we would neglect the richness of this person. Thus, I propose that we know this person in three kinds of narratives: historical narratives, the Gospels and biographies of exemplary Christians. By taking this threefold approach, we can respect the mystery of Christ while simultaneously adopting familiar forms of discourse.

A biography is not the last word about a person. It can prompt further discussion regarding the truth of this life and the nature of personal existence in general. To put this another way, narrative discourse provides only part of the answer to "Who is so-and-so?" It can be developed in more conceptual language—in language, for instance, that explicitly employs the ideas of person as agent, person as relation and person as subject. So too, talk about Jesus Christ does not stop with narratives. It assumes more discursive forms in which the use of clear notions of person sheds further light on Jesus Christ and the existence of all men and women.[54]

II.3 *Notions of Person in Christology*

The word "person" has a rich history in theology.[55] It appeared first in the writings of Tertullian and Hippolytus of Rome, and it increasingly functioned with technical precision in the evolution of theological controversies, doctrines and systematic theologies. In recent years major theologians have written theological anthropologies in which they reflect on the nature of personal existence and the reality of Jesus Christ. The works of Karl Rahner and Wolfhart Pannenberg, for example, have significant implications for Christology.[56] Here we will consider how the three notions of person that we treated in section one bear on our view of Jesus Christ.

Person as subject has played a primary role in some of the' most important theological investigations of the twentieth century. To break with the positivism of the nineteenth century, which in effect reduced persons to objects, many theologians have stressed human subjectivity. In this view, the self exists beyond the scope of scientific scrutiny. Personal existence entails self-consciousness, and personal identity concerns the self that is inaccessible to the scientist's and historian's detached observation. For Christology, this means that the identity of Jesus Christ evades historical inquiry. Jesus Christ is known indirectly through an intuitive grasp of personal existence in general. While all people are drawn to trust in the source of life, Jesus Christ has done this with complete self-abandon. He has totally surrendered himself to God, and therefore he has accomplished what the rest of us never fully realize apart from him, perfect union with God. This use of person as subject in Christology occurs in the work of Rahner and also in the new quest for the historical Jesus.

According to Rahner personal existence is characterized by subjectivity. We are persons in that we are knowing subjects. That is, we are capable of reflecting on ourselves and our involvements. In Rahner's words, "*spirit* is the single person insofar as he becomes conscious of himself in an absolute presence to himself . . . "[57] In light of this subjectivity, God calls each of us to become a full self, one who says yes to self, to God, and to neighbor. We hesitate however to do this, for we fear the loss of control and the sense of falling into an "abyss." Yet, Jesus Christ has responded to God's call with his whole self. In his life, passion and death, he has totally accepted himself as subject, as a self relating to self, God and others, and in his resurrection he has received the fullness of life. Therefore, Jesus Christ is the "absolute Savior," the one with whom we can be united so as also to become full subjects before God.

Person as subject does not of course stand alone in Rahner's writings. In his ecclesiology Rahner emphasizes person as relation, and in his later Christology he accentuates the historical Jesus' words and deeds, thereby implicitly employing person as agent.[58] Nevertheless, Rahner makes extensive use of person as subject because it aligns with his understanding of God as mystery. The self relating to itself and freely accepting its subjectivity is united with God, the infinite mystery whose divine life is love, God's joyous self-giving. This theme is a major one in Rahner's writings, and therefore person as subject holds a central place in his thought.

Person as subject also plays a key role in the new quest. As noted earlier, Käsemann and the other new questers seek to uncover the material continuity between the historical Jesus and the Christ of faith. To do this, they highlight Jesus' abiding disposition—an attitude beneath the surface of his words and deeds—and then they show how this way of relating to life is also declared in the early Church's proclamation about the risen Christ. This approach depends therefore upon the view that the self is not primarily manifest in one's words and deeds, but in one's abiding outlook on life, an attitude that persists beneath the surface of one's activities.

James M. Robinson, for instance, presents the view of person as subject when he states that personal identity is not to be found in one's "*empirical habitus,*" that is, in dates, places and specific incidents. This positivism distorts the nature of personal existence. Who someone is is a matter of the self relating to itself, and in this dynamism making a commitment to a definite kind of life. The self is defined therefore by its abiding disposition, its basic decision to approach life in a particular way. Robinson writes:

> The self is not simply one's personality, resultant upon (and to be explained by) the various influences and ingredients pres-

ent in one's heritage and development. . . . Selfhood results
from implicit or explicit commitment to a kind of existence,
and is to be understood only in terms of that commitment, i.e.,
by laying hold of the understanding of existence in terms of
which the self is constituted.[59]

According to the new questers, Jesus' life was marked by his radical
trust in God, and therefore this reliance on God gives an indication of
Jesus' identity. Historical research has substantiated that Jesus of Nazareth spoke with an exceptional inner authority, addressed God as Abba,
and freely went to his death rather than betray his mission. These historical conclusions are clues to Jesus' basic attitude: he was motivated
by his unwavering faith in God, and this motivation lies at the core of
Jesus' person. Jesus is the person of utter dependence on God, and this
total trust is what characterizes Jesus before his death and after his resurrection. The material continuity between the historical Jesus and the
risen Christ is the attitude of abiding confidence in God. Thus Käsemann
states: "The Gospel is tied to [Jesus] who, both before and after Easter,
revealed himself to his own as the Lord, by setting them before the God
who is near to them and thus translating them into the freedom and responsibility of faith."[60] Jesus Christ is defined by his complete faith in
God, and he brings his followers to make a similar act of trust in the God
whom he calls Abba. Jesus' identity springs from his perfect relating to
himself and God, and he leads other men and women to become full
subjects before God.

Person as subject can indeed serve Christology well, as Rahner and
the new questers have demonstrated in their respective ways. It allows
us to appraise empirical analyses that might reduce Jesus Christ to an
historical figure, and it permits us to reflect on the quality of Jesus' bond
with God. Nevertheless, one liability of its use in Christology is its tendency toward dualism. Talk about persons as subjects can foster a hard
distinction between the object and the subject, between the phenomenal
and the real, so that we would distinguish between "inner" history and
"outer" history.

This tension has been noted, for example, in Rahner's writings. According to Metz, Rahner's transcendental method can be used to disre-
gard historical contingencies as well as the theological significance of
"*praxis.*"[61] This does not occur in Rahner's work, observes Metz, be-

cause Rahner writes with the Church's actual life in mind. Yet, this implicit reference to Church history is not required by the transcendental method, and on its own terms the method discounts the historical character of God's revelation.

The possible devaluing of history in the language of subjectivity has significant implications for answering "Who is Jesus Christ?" When person as subject governs our discourse, we can have difficulty identifying a person. Since person as subject focuses on a person's abiding disposition and regards a person's words and actions as mere indicators of this attitude, it can make too little of biography's role in our knowledge of other persons. Then when this view is extended to Christology, it has difficulty saying who Jesus Christ is, for it places a great deal of weight on his total trust in God—a trust that all men and women should adopt. As a result, person as subject can lead us to misconstrue Jesus Christ as merely a token or symbol of what all people can become.

In recent years the work of Käsemann, Robinson and others has received criticism for this very reason. It is argued that their approach to history, the "new historiography," has resulted in the blurring of Jesus Christ's individuality. Leander Keck has pointed out, for instance, that the new quest casts Jesus as "the embodiment of the existentialist message."[62] What is important is not Jesus Christ himself, but his call for reliance on God. In a similar vein, Hans Frei maintains that the kind of "identity analysis" undertaken by the post-Bultmannians either loses sight of a person or posits a person's identity in an "unswerving inward disposition" that is so "inward" that the self cannot be known by others.[63] Each of us is estranged from our neighbor, even from those who love us and want to know us. This view of personal existence is problematic, and the difficulty stems from the new quest's emphasis upon person as subject.

Person as subject need not govern Christology. Person as agent and person as relation shape the Christologies of Kasper, Schillebeeckx and van Beeck, even though these approaches to Jesus Christ differ in other ways. For example, Schillebeeckx espouses person as agent, when he maintains that "it is only in his actions that a man is finally to be understood."[64] Moreover, he stresses person as relation, when he states that "an individual human being is the personal focal point of a series of interactive relations to the past, the future and his or her own present."[65] Further: "In other words, being a person entails interpersonality."[66] Finally, Schillebeeckx has stressed person as agent and person as relation without disregarding person as subject. He acknowledges, for example, the link between person as agent and person as subject in this statement: "Now the mystery of each person is only accessible to us in his behaviour, which on the other hand is just the inadequate sign of the person manifesting himself in it and at the same time conceals him."[67] Similarly, in their works Kasper and van Beeck accentuate person as agent and person as relation, while not losing sight of person as subject.

The adoption of person as agent and person as relation in Christology may appear, however, to pose a dilemma. How can these notions be employed when a biography of Jesus is neither in fact possible nor in principle theologically sufficient? To advocate primary reliance on person as agent and person as relation in Christology seems to demand a return to the original quest with its attempt to write a biography of Jesus. But this does not in fact occur in the Christologies of Kasper, Schillebeeckx and van Beeck. These theologians have relied on person as agent and person as relation without reverting to the liberal agenda. How has this been possible?

Analysis will show that Kasper, Schillebeeckx and van Beeck have turned to forms of narrative other than biography. Kasper's *Jesus the Christ* implicitly rests on an historical narrative of Jesus and also on biblical stories. Schillebeeckx's *Jesus* depends on an historical narrative, and van Beeck's *Christ Proclaimed* is undergird by the "Synoptic story," the drama running through Gospels of Matthew, Mark and Luke. Further, these accounts manifest person as agent in that Jesus stands out as the individual who enacts his intention to live faithfully to God, and person as relation functions in these accounts for Jesus Christ is presented as the individual who totally gives and receives from God and neighbor. One of the significant contributions made by Kasper, Schillebeeckx and van Beeck to recent Christology consists of their reliance on narratives and the ideas of person as agent and person as relation.

Biographies of Christians are not however employed in the Christologies of Kasper, Schillebeeckx and van Beeck, and it is here that I shall expand their use of narratives. Study of the person and work of Jesus Christ draws not only on historical data, Scripture and tradition, but also on contemporary experience. This experience is probed by Kasper, Schillebeeckx and van Beeck through their distinct analyses of modern thought. Yet there are other ways of learning from Christians' living encounter with Christ. One such source, as Kasper has noted, is the Church's liturgy. Another, mentioned by Metz, is the lives of the saints, especially those women and men whose discipleship to Christ has included their critical integration of the Christian heritage and their culture. Among exemplary twentieth century Christians in the United States stands Dorothy Day (d. 1980), and therefore a biographical sketch of Day can serve as a source for Christology. I shall demonstrate this in an inquiry into the identity of Jesus Christ that employs an historical narrative about Jesus, a retelling of Mark's Gospel, and a recollection of Day's life.

Finally, our examination of the works of Kasper, Schillebeeckx and van Beeck (Chapters Two, Three and Four), along with an exercise in identifying Jesus Christ (Chapter Five), positions us to consider the rationale for the use of narratives in Christology (Chapter Six). This rationale can be presented in three points. First, just as the lives of all persons are similar to narratives, so too the "life" of Christ is like a narrative that is glimpsed, for instance, when Christians profess: "Christ has died; Christ is risen; Christ will come again." Second, Christ's life is too complex to gain adequate expression in only one kind of narrative. Therefore, it can be recounted in historical reconstructions, the Gospels and the lives of the saints. Third, narratives about a life need not block other kinds of discourse about a person, and they can in fact clarify our use of conceptual terms. As a result, by employing narratives in Christology, we can recover the meaning of the Church's teachings about Jesus Christ.

III. *Myth, Story and History*

Talk about narratives can easily become tangled. The word "narrative" and its related terms can mean such different things that, unless these words are defined, what they mean can be ambiguous. Therefore, before going any further, I shall clarify the meaning of "myth," "history" and "story." Each of these terms specifies a distinct form of narrative. A narrative is "a recital of events."[68] It is an account with "a beginning, a middle and an end."[69] Having recognized this much, we need to distinguish among some of the different kinds of narrative.

"Myth" refers to that kind of narrative which recounts "events" outside of time—"events" in which we can participate through rituals. The Bible's two creation accounts (Genesis 1 and Genesis 2) are myths, as is the Greek tale of Prometheus. These narratives are such that they can provide people of every age with a sense of the meaning of their basic involvements. Norman Perrin makes this point when he states: "Myths are narratives that express in symbolically rich language human experiences that resist expression in any objective, descriptive language."[70] Because myths express recurring experiences, they are characterized by their circularity. Or, in the words of William Poteat, a myth is distinguished by the fact that:

> though, like a story it unfolds in time, so that in one perfectly good sense we may say there are "events" recounted . . . and we may say that these "events" are laid out in time, so that, in one sense, we want to claim that Y was *after* X and *before* Z . . . it is not a report of unique events, and, in *our* senses of these notions, has neither a beginning nor an end—as a circle has neither a beginning nor an end.[71]

"Story" denotes that kind of narrative whose events as reported occur once and for all. It is a drama whose beginning, a middle and an end are indeed just that, and not moments within a cycle. Moreover, a story consists of characters who are singular, not archetypes as in a myth. Poteat states:

> A *story* is a temporal deployment of events which differs from myth, in the Classical sense, in that it requires the concept "happen" in a logical environment other than that afforded by ritual re-enactment, the passage of the cosmos through its finite course and eternal return; it requires the concept "person"; and it requires that of "action."[72]

Moreover, the category story can be divided into two sub-categories. There are fictional stories.[73] These stories are "made up"; that is, their events and characters are invented by the storyteller. Examples of fiction are Fyodor Dostoyevski's *The Brothers Karamazov* (1879), Mark Twain's *The Adventures of Huckleberry Finn* (1884), and Willa Cather's *My Antonia* (1918). Yet, there are also non-fictional stories.[74]

These stories possess a real subject matter. They speak of actual events and persons, in such a way that, while they manifest historical accuracy, they primarily aim at providing insight into the essential human ingredients in this drama. Hence, in non-fictional stories the storyteller fills in historical gaps with imagined elements. An example of a non-fiction story in contemporary literature is Truman Capote's novel *In Cold Blood* (1965). In ancient literature, the Gospels of Matthew, Mark, Luke and John can be classified as non-fiction stories, even though they are a genre unto themselves.

Finally, "history" refers to that type of narrative which is intended to possess empirical or historical accuracy in speaking of actual events and persons. Thus, according to Poteat: "*History* is a similar temporal deployment of events [—similar to story—], bound to what we question-beggingly, but unproblematically, and . . . benignly call 'facts.' "[75] Or, as Warner Berthoff states, history "is meant to reveal a preexistent order of actuality."[76]

These descriptions should help us to keep our wits about us as we consider the use of narratives in Christology. It can be immediately clarified, for instance, that we are not interested in myths. It may be that some biblical stories function in the Church's life as myths would, for example, by shaping ritual activity. Yet, such narratives as the Gospels are not myths, but non-fiction stories. In subsequent pages, I shall argue that Christology can benefit from the explicit use of the Gospels as stories, historical narratives about Jesus (that is, from loose recitals of actual persons and events in Jesus' ministry), and biographies of exemplary Christians.

Christians have always inquired into the identity of Jesus Christ, and in recent years we have done this with exceptional vigor. Paul VI in 1963 exhorted the delegates at the Second Vatican Council to set their deliberations in relation to Jesus Christ, and in 1979 John Paul II directed the entire Church to describe itself within the mystery of Christ. Toward this, he envisioned the Church as "the community of disciples."[77] Along with Church leaders, theologians have taken a serious interest in Christology. Influenced by modern historical methods and philosophy as well as by cultural issues, they have studied anew the incarnation, Jesus' life and ministry, the resurrection, the kerygma's emergence, and the present and future reality of Christ. In the past thirty years, the Christian assembly has embarked upon what Aloys Grillmeier has predicted will prove to be a new "Christological age."[78]

Walter Kasper has consistently contributed to our era of Christology. In *Jesus the Christ, The God of Jesus Christ* and numerous articles he has enriched our understanding of the person whom Christians confess as Lord. Moreover, his work is significant not only for its content, its view of Jesus Christ, but also for its form, its theological method. This method strikes a balance in its reliance on various theological sources, for it unites historical-critical research, the analysis of Christian kerygma and doctrines, and critical reliance on contemporary thought. It is displayed most clearly in *Jesus the Christ,* and therefore this is the work upon which we shall focus in the next chapter. Throughout our study, Kasper's "method of reciprocity" will serve as the primary paradigm for critical reflection upon the person and work of Jesus Christ.

NOTES

1. Paul VI, "The Opening Address at the Second Session of the Second Vatican Council" (September 29, 1963), in: Xavier Rynne, *The Second Session* (New York: Farrar, Straus and Company, 1963), pp. 347–363, 351.

2. John Paul II, *The Redeemer of Man* (Washington, D.C.: United States Catholic Conference, 1983), #7, p. 20.

3. *Ibid.,* #10, p. 29.

4. *Ibid.,* #21, p. 90.

5. Gerald O'Collins, *What Are They Saying About Jesus?,* second edition (New York: Paulist Press, 1983), p. 1. Cf. International Theological Commission, *Select Questions on Christology* (Washington, D.C.: United States Catholic Conference, 1980), p. 1.

6. Helpful introductions to recent Christology include: Gerald O'Collins, *Interpreting Jesus* (New York: Paulist Press, 1983); Walter Kasper, "Christologie und Anthropologie," *Theologische Quartalschrift,* CLXIII (1982), 202–221; Brian McDermott, "Roman Catholic Christology," *Theological Studies,* XLI (1980), 339–367; Francis Schüssler Fiorenza, "Christology After Vatican II," *The Ecumenist,* XVIII (1980), 81–89; John P. Galvin, "Jesus' Approach to Death," *Theological Studies,* XL (1980), 713–744; *idem,* "The Resurrection of Jesus in Contemporary Catholic Systematics," *The Heythrop Journal,* XX (1979), 123–145; Dietrich Wiederkehr, "Christologie im Kontext," in: Josef

Pfammatter (ed.), *Theologische Berichte VII* (Zurich: Benziger Verlag, 1978), pp. 11–68.

7. In stressing the question of Jesus' identity, I stand with Dietrich Bonhoeffer, *Christ the Center,* trans. J. Bowden (New York: Harper and Row, 1966), p. 30. This emphasis in Christology is discussed by Walter Lowe, "Christ and Salvation," in: Peter C. Hodgson and Robert H. King (eds.), *Christian Theology,* revised edition (Philadelphia: Fortress Press, 1985), pp. 222–248.

8. Johannes B. Metz, "Theology Today," *The Proceedings of the Catholic Theological Society of America,* XL (1985), pp. 1–14; *idem,* "An Identity Crisis in Christianity?" in: William Kelly (ed.), *Theology and Discovery* (Milwaukee: Marquette University Press, 1980), pp. 169–178; *idem, Faith in History and Society,* trans. D. Smith (New York: The Seabury Press, 1980), pp. 205–218 [first published in *Concilium,* IX (1973), pp. 84–96].

9. David Tracy, *The Analogical Imagination* (New York: Crossroad, 1981), pp. 275–281; *idem, Blessed Rage for Order* (New York: The Seabury Press, 1975), pp. 204–236.

10. Hans W. Frei, *The Identity of Jesus Christ* (Philadelphia: Fortress Press, 1975).

11. Avery Dulles, *Models of Revelation* (Garden City: Doubleday and Company, 1983), pp. 131–154.

12. George Stroup, *The Promise of Narrative Theology* (Atlanta: John Knox Press, 1981); John Navone and Thomas Cooper, *Tellers of the Word* (New York: LeJacq Publishers, 1981); Michael Goldberg, *Theology and Narrative* (Nashville: Abingdon Press, 1982); Terrence Tilley, *Story Theology* (Wilmington: Michael Glazier, 1985); Ronald F. Thiemann, *Revelation and Theology* (Notre Dame: University of Notre Dame Press, 1986). Cf. John Navone, "Narrative Theology: A Survey," *The Irish Theological Quarterly,* LII (1986), 212–230.

13. Walter Kasper, *Jesus the Christ,* trans. V. Green (New York: Paulist Press, 1976), pp. 15–25.

14. Edward Schillebeeckx, *Jesus,* trans. H. Hoskins (New York: The Seabury Press, 1979), pp. 105–398.

15. Frans Jozef van Beeck, *Christ Proclaimed* (New York: Paulist Press, 1979), pp. 358–375.

16. Cf. David Burrell, "Argument in Theology: Analogy and Narrative," in: Carl Raschke (ed.), *New Dimensions in Philosophical Theology* (Chico: Scholars Press, 1982), pp. 37–51.

17. Cf. Amelie Oksenberg Rorty (ed.), *The Identities of Persons* (Berkeley: University of California Press, 1976); John Perry (ed.), *Personal Identity* (Berkeley: University of California Press, 1975; Terence Penelhum, "Personal Identity," in: Paul Edwards (ed.), *The Encyclopedia of Philosophy,* VI (New York: Macmillan Publishing Company, 1967), pp. 95–107.

18. John R. Searle, "Proper Names and Descriptions," in: P. Edwards (ed.), *The Encyclopedia of Philosophy,* VI, pp. 487–491.

19. Hannah Arendt, *The Human Condition* (Chicago: University of Chicago Press, 1958), p. 186.

20. On the importance of context for understanding a person, see: Stuart Hampshire, *Thought and Action,* new edition (Notre Dame: University of Notre Dame Press, 1982), pp. 11–89.

21. Cf. Samuel H. Baron and Carl Pletsch (eds.), *Introspection in Biography* (Hillsdale, New Jersey: Analytic Press, 1985).

22. Cf. Robert H. King, *The Meaning of God* (Philadelphia: Fortress Press, 1973), pp. 7–13.

23. Frei, *The Identity of Jesus Christ,* p. 37.

24. Cf. Hampshire, *Thought and Action,* pp. 125–127.

25. Sydney Shoemaker, "Personal Identity," in: J. Perry (ed.), *Personal Identity,* pp. 119–134, 123.

26. Schillebeeckx, *Jesus,* p. 44; cf. *idem, Interim Report,* trans. J. Bowden (New York: Crossroad, 1981), pp. 67–68.

27. Richard Taylor, *Metaphysics,* third edition (Englewood Cliffs: Prentice-Hall, Inc., 1983), p. 116.

28. *Ibid.,* p. 14.

29. Bernard Williams, "The Self and the Future," in: Perry (ed.), *Personal Identity,* pp. 179–198.

30. Schillebeeckx, *Jesus,* p. 44.

31. John Perry, "The Problem of Personal Identity," in: *idem* (ed.), *Personal Identity,* pp. 3–32.

32. Cf. Wolfhart Pannenberg, *What Is Man?,* trans. D. A. Priebe (Philadelphia: Fortress Press, 1970), p. 139; *idem, Jesus—God and Man,* trans. L. Wilkins and D. Priebe (Philadelphia: The Westminster Press, 1968), p. 304, n. 59.

33. Stroup, *The Promise of Narrative Theology,* pp. 100–118, 111.

34. Stephen Crites, "The Narrative Quality of Experience," *The Journal of the American Academy of Religion,* XXXIX (1971), 291–311, 302.

35. King, *The Meaning of God* (Philadelphia: Fortress Press, 1973), pp. 21–48; *idem,* "The Conceivability of God," *Religious Studies,* IX (1973), pp. 11–22.

36. Charles Taylor, *Human Agency and Language,* I (Cambridge: Cambridge University Press, 1985), pp. 15–44, 97–114; Lawrence Davis, *Theory of Action* (Englewood Cliffs: Prentice-Hall, Inc., 1979).

37. Cornelius van Peursen, *Body, Soul, Spirit* (London: Oxford University Press, 1966), p. 147.

38. *Ibid.,* p. 153.

39. Arendt, *The Human Condition,* p. 179.

40. John Macmurray, *The Self as Agent* (Atlantic Highlands: Humanities Press, 1978), p. 90.

41. Martin Buber, *I and Thou*, second edition, trans. W. Kaufmann (New York: Scribners, 1970).

42. John Macmurray, *Persons in Relation* (Atlantic Highlands: Humanities Press, 1961), p. 17.

43. Ludwig Wittgenstein, *Tractatus Logico-Philosophicus* (New York: Humanities Press, 1961), 5.632–5.641. Cf. King, *The Meaning of God*, pp. 21–26.

44. Martin Heidegger, *Being and Time*, trans. J. Macquarrie and E. Robinson (New York: Harper and Row, 1962), p. 150.

45. Tracy, *The Analogical Imagination*, p. 408.

46. David Burrell, *Analogy and Philosophical Language* (New Haven: Yale University Press, 1973), p. 20.

47. Schillebeeckx, *Interim Report*, pp. 21–27.

48. O'Collins, *Interpreting Jesus*, pp. 47–49; Norman Perrin and Dennis Duling, *Introduction to the New Testament*, second edition (San Diego: Harcourt Brace Jovanovich, 1982), pp. 397–430.

49. Schillebeeckx, *Jesus*, p. 77.

50. Norman Perrin, *Rediscovering the Teaching of Jesus* (New York: Harper and Row, 1976), p. 214.

51. *Ibid.*, p. 220.

52. Ernst Käsemann, "The Problem of the Historical Jesus," in: *idem, Essays on New Testament Themes*, trans. W. J. Montaque (London: SCM Press, 1964), pp. 15–47, 46.

53. Perrin, *Rediscovering the Teaching of Jesus*, p. 226.

54. Cf. Donald MacKinnon, " 'Substance' in Christology," in: Stephen Sykes and J. P. Clayton (eds.), *Christ, Faith and History* (Cambridge: Cambridge University Press, 1973), pp. 279–300.

55. On "person" in Christology, see: Walter Kasper, *The God of Jesus Christ*, trans. M.J. O'Connell (New York: Crossroad, 1984), pp. 152–157, *passim; idem, Jesus the Christ*, pp. 240–252; Pannenberg, *Jesus—God and Man, passim.*

56. Karl Rahner, *Foundations of Christian Faith*, trans. W. Dych (New York: The Seabury Press, 1978), pp. 24–137; Wolfhart Pannenberg, *Anthropology in a Theological Perspective*, trans. M. O'Connell (Philadelphia: Fortress Press, 1985).

57. Rahner, *Foundations of Christian Faith*, p. 183.

58. *Ibid.*, pp. 246–249, 342–346. Cf. John M. McDermott, "The Christologies of Karl Rahner," *Gregorianum*, LXII #1 (1986), 87–123; *idem*, "The Christologies of Rahner - II," *Gregorianum*, LXII #2 (1986), 297–327.

59. James M. Robinson, *A New Quest of the Historical Jesus* (London: SCM Press, 1959), p. 67. Cf. Paul J. Achtemeir, *An Introduction to the New Hermeneutics* (Philadelphia: The Westminster Press, 1969).

60. Käsemann, "The Problem of the Historical Jesus," p. 46.

61. Metz, "An Identity Crisis in Christianity?" pp. 170–173; *idem*, "Karl Rahner—ein theologisches Leben," *Stimmen der Zeit*, CXCII (1974), 305–316. Cf. Robert Krieg, "The Crucified in Rahner's Christology," *The Irish Theological Quarterly*, L (1983/84), pp. 151–167.

62. Leander Keck, *A Future for the Historical Jesus*, revised edition (Nashville: Abingdon Press, 1981), pp. 122, 215–218.

63. Frei, *The Identity of Jesus Christ*, p. 88. According to Norman Perrin, we lack the historical data to accomplish what the new quest calls for; cf. Perrin, *Rediscovering the Teaching of Jesus*, p. 232.

64. Schillebeeckx, *Jesus*, p. 258; cf. p. 78.

65. *Ibid.*, p. 44.

66. *Ibid.*, p. 662.

67. *Ibid.*, p. 259.

68. William H. Poteat, "Myths, Stories, History, Eschatology and Action," in: Thomas Langford and W. Poteat (eds.), *Intellect and Hope* (Durham: Duke University Press, 1968), pp. 198–231, 220. Cf. Robert Scholes and Robert Kellogg, *The Nature of Narrative* (London: Oxford University Press, 1966).

69. Arthur C. Danto, *Analytical Philosophy of History* (Cambridge: Cambridge University Press, 1965), p. 233.

70. Perrin and Duling, *The New Testament*, p. 51.

71. Poteat, "Myths, Stories, History . . . ," pp. 221–222.

72. *Ibid.*, p. 226.

73. Warner Berthoff, "Fiction, History, Myth: Notes Toward the Discrimination of Narrative Forms," in: *idem, Fiction and Events* (New York: E. P. Dutton, 1971), pp. 30–55, 37.

74. David H. Kelsey, "Appeals to Scripture in Theology," *The Journal of Religion*, XLVIII (1968), 1–21, 12; *idem, The Uses of Scripture in Recent Theology* (Philadelphia: Fortress Press, 1975), p. 48.

75. Poteat, "Myths, Stories, History . . . ," p. 226.

76. Berthoff, "Fiction, History, Myth," p. 40.

77. John Paul II, *The Redeemer of Man*, #21, p. 90.

78. Aloys Grillmeier, "The Figure of Christ in Catholic Theology Today," in: Johannes Feiner *et al.* (eds.), *Theology Today:* Volume One, *The Renewal in Dogma*, trans. P. White and R.H. Kelly (Milwaukee: Bruce Publishing, 1965), pp. 66–108, 66.

Chapter Two

THREE SOURCES FOR CHRISTOLOGY

In 1983 Brother Roger Schutz, prior and founder of Taizé's ecumenical community, was asked how Christians can deepen their faith. In response he urged the discovery of the living Christ. Brother Roger stated:

> If they could see that the greatest mystery, the most profound and generous of all, is the Risen Christ present for every human being without exception, then maybe they would understand why the main thing in life is our friendship with Christ, our confidence in Him. Because He is risen, He is present for all. Whether they recognize Him or not, He suffers with all who suffer, He weeps with all who weep. He goes through agony with all in agony, He rejoices with all who rejoice. When we glimpse this reality, then welcoming Christ into our life becomes the one thing that really matters.[1]

Brother Roger's view of the risen Christ is assuring: The Lord abides with us. Moreover, it awakens the desire to know this "person" better: Who is this who suffers when we suffer, and rejoices when we rejoice? Direct knowledge of Jesus Christ occurs of course primarily through prayer and discipleship. But we can also learn about him through systematic inquiry. A fuller understanding of the risen Christ can develop as we order and appraise the Christian community's experience, images and ideas of Christ. Such is the task of Christology.

Christology's main goal, says Walter Kasper, is to identify Jesus Christ. It gives primacy to the question "Who is Jesus Christ?" To put this another way, it expresses the meaning of the Christian assembly's convictions regarding the "Lord." In Kasper's words: "The assertion

'Jesus is the Christ' is the basic statement of Christian belief, and Christology is no more than the conscientious elucidation of that proposition.''[2] If we want therefore to understand more clearly the person to whom Brother Roger has referred, we can turn to Christology—at least Christology of the sort done by Kasper.

More than a decade has passed since the publication of Kasper's *Jesus the Christ*. Since 1974, the Tübingen theologian has written *The God of Jesus Christ* (1984) and numerous other scholarly texts.[3] Further, he has edited the German bishops' adult catechism and, in the autumn of 1985, he served as the theological secretary for the extraordinary synod of bishops in Rome. Through these involvements, Kasper has sustained his Christological interest and refined some aspects of his thought, for example, on the Holy Spirit.[4] As a result, the book that began as lectures at the universities of Münster and Tübingen during the late 1960's and early 1970's is now somewhat dated.[5] Nevertheless, *Jesus the Christ* stands as a major contribution to contemporary Christology, for not only does it offer rich insights into the person and work of Jesus Christ, it also demonstrates a balanced approach to this living reality.

Both the content and form of *Jesus the Christ* are worth serious study.[6] In Kasper's view Jesus is "the mediator between God and man."[7] He is the reconciler who has healed the rift between God and the world, thereby "releasing" the Holy Spirit throughout history so that all of creation can be united to God. This view of Jesus Christ is reinforced by the book's method. Kasper is intent not only on presenting Christ as the mediator, but also on arriving at this perception in a way that reconciles the modern split between faith and reason. Since the Enlightenment, observes the Tübingen theologian, we have experienced a dichotomy between Christian belief and scientific knowledge.[8] Yet, if in fact Jesus Christ is the bearer of unity, then there must be a way to reflect on him that is itself unifying. This theological method cannot therefore be either narrowly rational, according to the Enlightenment's norms, or strictly confessional, "fideistic." Rather it must be a method of reconciliation, of "reciprocity." Given its complementarity of content and form, *Jesus the Christ* exhibits what it talks about: a theology of mediation.[9]

The value of *Jesus the Christ* derives in large part from its breadth, its catholicity.[10] The Christ it speaks of is not simply the result of historical study, nor is he solely an interpretation of the doctrine of Chalcedon, nor is he only the embodiment of recent Christian experience. This Christ has emerged from all three sources: historical research, Scripture and tradition, and the Church's current life.[11] He is a multi-dimensional figure in whom diverse and seemingly disparate kinds of material are brought together. In sum, the validity of *Jesus the Christ* stems from its tapping of Christian belief's major wellsprings.

One intriguing feature of *Jesus the Christ* is its implicit reliance on narratives that are found in its sources. One such narrative runs throughout Kasper's historical review of Jesus' ministry. It is comparable to a rough biographical sketch of Jesus. A second kind of narrative operates in Kasper's systematic reflections upon the risen Christ. In speaking about Jesus as "Son of God," "son of man," and "mediator," Kasper refers to scriptural stories—for example, to the servant hymn of Philippians 2:6–8 and to the motif of the new Adam in Romans 5:12–21. In analyzing *Jesus the Christ,* I shall argue that these narratives could be made more explicit so that they clarify the more theoretical statements about Jesus Christ.[12]

Jesus the Christ consists of three major sections. In the first, "Jesus Christ Today," Kasper explains his theological method. In the second, "The History and Destiny of Jesus Christ," he reviews Jesus' life and Christian testimony about his resurrection. In the third section, "The Mystery of Jesus Christ," he reflects on the risen Christ as the obedient Son, the new man, and the mediator between God and creation. My discussion of Kasper's text treats each of its three major sections.

I.1 *The Centrality of the Risen Christ*

Christology, says Kasper, is directed toward the identity of an individual. It includes the study of this person's work or "cause," but it does not separate his work from his person. Such a split occurs in the writings of Willi Marxsen, and at times it crops up in Hans Küng's *On Being a Christian.*[13] But, for Kasper, Jesus' cause must be linked with his person, and conversely his person with his cause or mission. Further, while Christology illuminates the nature and destiny of all humankind, it does this in the light received by turning primarily to Jesus Christ. Inquiry into the person and work of Jesus Christ is distinct from, though related to, study of what it means to be human. Christology and theological anthropology are closely bound in the writings of Karl Rahner, and this can be misconstrued (contrary to Rahner's intention), observes Kasper, to mean that Jesus Christ is merely a token of what all people can become.[14] To avoid this misreading, Kasper keeps posing forms of the identity question: "Who is Jesus Christ? Who is Jesus Christ for us today?" "Where and how do we meet Jesus Christ today?" "The decisive question for Christianity has always been 'Who do you think Christ is? Who is he?'"[15]

This insistence on the identity of Jesus Christ is prompted by both theological and philosophical reasons. The theological rationale concerns the centrality of Jesus' death and resurrection for understanding his person and work. The philosophical rationale highlights our human condition in general and our longing for freedom. Each of these needs to be elucidated.

According to Kasper the full revelation of Jesus Christ occurred at Easter. While Jesus was disclosed in his words and deeds throughout his ministry, he was completely revealed as he suffered, died and rose from the dead. Because of this, any attempts to inquire into his identity must direct attention to Jesus' death and resurrection. The effort to understand Jesus cannot bracket testimony to his Easter appearances and empty tomb. Rather, Christology must begin with an early, simple Easter proclamation: "Jesus is the Christ" (Jn 20:31; cf. Phil 2:11; Mk 8:29; Acts 2:26). "According to Scripture," observes Kasper, "Christology has its centre in the cross and the Resurrection."[16]

This emphasis on the risen Christ highlights the inadequacy of a solely historical starting point in Christology. To be true to its subject matter, Christology recognizes at the outset that Jesus Christ is not only located within our matrix of time and space. Its primary question is posed not solely in the past tense—i.e., Who *was* Jesus?—but also in the present tense—i.e., Who *is* Jesus? Thus Kasper writes:

> Nevertheless it is impossible to make the historical Jesus the entire and only valid content of faith in Christ. For revelation occurs not only in the earthly Jesus, but just as much, more indeed, in the Resurrection and the imparting of the Spirit. Jesus today is living 'in the Spirit'. Hence we are granted not only an historically mediated, but direct mode of access to Jesus Christ 'in the Spirit'.[17]

The centrality of the resurrection means further that Christology must be done within the Church. Our knowledge of Jesus Christ rests on the testimony of the apostles. In Kasper's words: "Jesus of Nazareth is accessible for us only by way of the faith of the first Christian churches."[18] Moreover, Christology must be grounded in the Church's living witness to Christ. Again, to quote Kasper: "We should not remove the Jesus tradition from the context of proclamation, liturgy and parish practice of the Christian churches."[19] Knowledge of Jesus Christ must be anchored in the believing community's testimony, that is, both in its early kerygma and in its current preaching.

Complementing this theological perspective on Jesus Christ is Kasper's more philosophical position. Throughout his work the Tübingen theologian refers to the French philosopher Blaise Pascal (d. 1662). In particular, he frequently quotes the *Pensees,* #397: "The greatness of man is great because he knows his own misery." This sober assessment of the human condition is more accurate, notes Kasper, than the more optimistic view of the French philosopher Maurice Blondel (d. 1949) whose thought influenced important twentieth century theologian Karl Rahner.[20] Having matured during the Second World War and its holocaust, Kasper agrees with thinkers like Pascal who recognize human limits and evil in the world, and in light of this he stresses our dilemma: We want to become free, and yet we cannot realize this *telos* through our own efforts. Our frustration and pain alert us to our high aspirations and simultaneously to our finitude as well as to the demonic in creation.[21]

This appraisal of our situation has led Kasper beyond the Enlightenment and German Idealism, with their naive trust in human reason, to post-Enlightenment thought. Since he works within the German context, Kasper has looked within his heritage for appropriate philosophical resources and has found a major source in the later work of F. W. J. Schelling (d. 1854).[22] In his early years Schelling significantly contributed to the emergence of German Idealism, which G. W. F. Hegel (d. 1831) then crafted into a complete "system" of thought—a system that put an end to the Enlightenment. But having planted the seeds of German Idealism, Schelling also repudiated its full growth, for he came to realize that knowledge of human ways of knowing and consciousness is not complete in itself. The life of the mind must reach toward the reality of history and ultimately toward *the* reality (God or "the Absolute") revealed in history. With Schelling, Kasper holds a key conviction: We cannot think out history, we must live it out.[23] We need to become enlightened therefore about the limits of the Enlightenment and Idealism. When we do so, we will have reached what Kasper calls the "Second Enlightenment"—a position similar to what Theodore Adorno, Jurgen Habermas and Max Horkheimer of the Frankfurt School term "the dialectic of the Enlightenment."[24]

According to Kasper, philosophies of the sort advocated by the later Schelling in the nineteenth century and by the Frankfurt School in the twentieth century point beyond themselves. They remind us that as we uncover our yearning for emancipation from all limits and evil, we face our inability to fulfill this profound desire. At this existential juncture, we confront an "either/or." Either we despair, or we look in history for a moment when something radically new was introduced into creation, when a liberating element or person entered into our circumscribed setting. If such an "event" had occurred in history, it would assure us that we had already been "saved" and thus that our longing for freedom would be realized.[25]

The later Schelling saw the need for a new beginning in history. He judged that the human mind alone could not bring order and direction to the material world, but it needs to cooperate with a "potency" that has freely entered into history's creative process. This insight brought him to shift from "negative philosophy," which studies the structures of human cognition and consciousness, to "positive philosophy," which reflects on the human situation and destiny in a way that integrates Christian revelation and modern thought.[26]

What Schelling envisioned in his positive philosophy is not unlike what Kasper has undertaken in his theological investigations. Assuming the validity of the Church's prayers, creeds and doctrines, Kasper has sought to understand them anew in light of post-Enlightenment thought, especially with its emphasis on freedom. Kasper has undertaken what Anselm (d. 1109) has described in the *Proslogion* as "faith seeking understanding." Motivated by his realism about our human condition, Kasper concentrates on the new element that has come into history, Jesus Christ who is present in the Spirit to all people, and, focusing on this one point of hope, Kasper attempts to understand anew the Church's convictions and teachings about this Christ.[27]

To sum up, two kinds of reasoning lead to Kasper's emphasis upon the identity of Jesus Christ. One is theological: Jesus is fully revealed in his death and resurrection, and, in response to this disclosure, the early Church acclaimed that Jesus is the Christ. This is the point therefore from which we can appropriately begin an inquiry about this person—a person who is not solely a past figure but also a present and future reality. The other rationale is philosophical: in the twentieth century we have come face-to-face with finitude and evil, and in this gap we must search in history for the arrival of the one person who has answered creation's longing for freedom. This is Jesus Christ, and thus critical thought about him is directed to shedding light on his person and work. These lines of theological and philosophical reasoning meet in Christology and direct it to one question: Who is Jesus Christ?

I.2 *"A Christology of Reciprocity"*

Christology has a primary task: to inquire into the identity of Jesus Christ. From one perspective, it possesses therefore a narrow focus, one person. Yet, from another vantage point, systematic study about Jesus Christ takes a broad focus, for it identifies this person by drawing on more than one source. It does not rely, for example, solely on historical data about him. According to Kasper, Christology depends on three distinct, though complementary sources: (1) the contemporary Church's life and thought, (2) historical investigation, and (3) the Jewish-Christian Scripture and tradition. These sources contribute to what Kasper calls "a Christology of reciprocity," an inquiry that reciprocates between "the earthly Jesus *and* the risen, exalted Christ."[28]

Theologians do not work in a vacuum, nor do they stand at some neutral point outside the Church. They participate in the Christian assembly, and this involvement influences their systematic study. In *The Methods of Dogmatic Theology,* Kasper declares: "No one starts from scratch. The heritage of tradition situates us within a very definite horizon of truth."[29] Theologians should not set their faith aside when they critically investigate theological issues. How can they, since their inquiries are motivated by faith? Thus, for instance, in *Jesus the Christ,* Kasper states: "The starting point of Christology is the phenomenology of faith in Christ; faith as it is actually believed, lived, proclaimed and practised in the Christian churches."[30] One source for Christology is therefore the Christian community in which theologians worship, serve and study.

This source ought not however be reduced to a non-thinking form of piety. Participation in the believing community entails the critical adoption of an era's thought. This means that the issues and ideas of an epoch shape theologians' reflections on Jesus Christ. Quite concretely, theologians bring these questions and concepts to their research into Christology's other sources, namely to history, Scripture and tradition. In our era, Kasper notes, the most pressing concern is that of freedom.[31] In Christology, the modern interest in liberation is located in the issue of Jesus' particularity and universality.[32]

According to the Enlightenment persons and events cannot have timeless significance, because they are contingent.[33] They depend upon such universal principles as the law of gravity, laws of probability, and psychological types. Persons and events make a cosmic impact insofar as they manifest a natural principle or ahistorical idea, and in this case they function only as a cipher or token of something else. They are not intrinsically linked to what they embody. For example, in an Enlightenment view Moses' exodus from Egypt is not a special disclosure of God, but an expression of the longing for independence that stirs in all peoples. Or, to take another instance, Jesus' life and destiny attests not to God's intervention in human affairs, but to the human potential for goodness and a fullness of life that threatens the reality of death. In an Enlightenment view, therefore, very little can be claimed for specific persons and events since they result from universal ideas and laws.

This outlook is ultimately imprisoning. It regards persons and events as determined by inflexible principles, and in light of such twentieth century experiences as the two world wars and the holocaust, the Enlightenment view extinguishes the flame of freedom that burns within human hearts. In Kasper's judgment the problematic of timeless truths and historical change can be resolved only from a post-Enlightenment position, along the lines envisioned by the later Schelling. The desire for freedom awakened by the Enlightenment cannot be adequately understood in the Enlightenment's categories. Therefore, a new language must develop that enables us to speak about history's possibilities, and this language can be shaped by Christian theologians in light of Jesus' life, death and resurrection.

Freedom is therefore a major issue that today's Christian theologians bring to an inquiry into the reality of Jesus Christ. Concurring with Johann Baptist Metz, Kasper declares:

> Emancipation is to be seen as a kind of epochal catchword for our present experience of the world and as an historical-philosophical category for the process of enlightenment and freedom in the modern era, in the circumstances (and not just the conditions) of which we have to articulate and represent the Christian message of redemption (Metz).[34]

One source for Christology is the contemporary Church's life and thought, and in our day this experience involves in large part the issue of freedom. It prompts us to ask: How can our yearning for emancipation be fulfilled, since we cannot realize it on our own? Moreover, in what way has Jesus Christ introduced this freedom into history, and how can we talk about him without lapsing into the dichotomy between timeless truths and contingent events? With questions like these in mind, Kasper turns to two other sources for Christology.

Two other sources for Christology are indicated by an early form of the kerygma.[35] "Jesus is the Christ" (Jn 20:31) points to both the historical Jesus and the risen Christ. In this confession, "Jesus" refers to a past figure, the man who grew up in Nazareth, preached throughout Galilee, and was put to death in Jerusalem in approximately 30 C.E. Simultaneously, the confession's use of "the Christ" signifies a present and future reality, the individual who is fully united with God through the Holy Spirit. In light of this early kerygma, our efforts to identify Jesus Christ must look to both the findings of historians and also to the Christian assembly's Scripture and tradition.

On the one hand, systematic inquiry into the identity of Jesus Christ includes the results of historical-critical research. Theologians utilize historians' methods and conclusions in order to link their investigation to an historically contingent individual. Christology reconstructs this man's ministry, last days, death, and followers' responses to these events. In other words, it includes an historical narrative about Jesus. In Kasper's words:

[Christology] has to preserve a real and actual unique memory, and to represent it here and now. It has to narrate a real and actual story—history—and to bear testimony to it. It has to ask, in other words: Who was this Jesus of Nazareth? What did he want? What was his mission and message, his behaviour and destiny? What was (despite the dangers of the term) his 'cause'? How did this Jesus, who proclaimed not himself but the imminent Rule of God, become the proclaimed and believed-in Christ?[36]

On the other hand, Christology depends on the Church's Scripture and tradition. Knowledge of the risen Christ is a function of the believing community's faith. Christianity rests in part on the shoulders of its forebears, for example, on Peter, James, John, and the women. Therefore, Christology too draws on this source as expressed, for instance, in the early kerygma, the Scriptures, Church teachings and conciliar formulations. These documents witness in various ways to the Christian assembly's encounters with the exalted Lord. To quote Kasper: ''Jesus today is living 'in the Spirit'. Hence we are granted not only an historically mediated, but direct mode of access to Jesus Christ 'in the Spirit'.''[37] Because Jesus Christ is a living reality, Christians' testimony in every age, especially in the early Church, is a wellspring for Christology.

Three sources for Christology are therefore these: the contemporary Church's life and thought, careful historical research into Jesus' life and times, and Scripture and tradition. Each contributes to what Kasper calls a Christology of reciprocity, ''a Christology of complementarity,'' for each source is distinct from the others and yet fills out the others. Just how this can occur is demonstrated by Kasper as he undertakes his Christological investigation in the second and third major sections of *Jesus the Christ*. In section two, ''The History and Destiny of Jesus Christ,'' Kasper draws on contemporary Christians' concern for freedom and historical study about Jesus. In section three, ''The Mystery of Jesus Christ,'' Kasper simultaneously mines both the theme of liberation and also Scripture and tradition about Jesus Christ. This format shapes the remainder of this chapter.

II.1 *God's "New Start"*

In the second section of *Jesus the Christ* Kasper assembles a wealth of data about Jesus' ministry and times in order to argue that the historical Jesus was "a figure of unparalleled originality." Kasper states this thesis at the outset of "The History and Destiny of Jesus Christ":

> In the early years of this century, various theses were propounded which all assert that Jesus never lived, and that the story of Jesus is a myth or legend. These claims have long since been exposed as historical nonsense. . . . In addition, we can point to a general consensus among exegetes (who, in the last ten years particularly, have concentrated on the question of the historical Jesus), that the characteristics of the activity and preaching of Jesus stand out with relative clarity from the darkness of history. The Jesus we have as a result is *a figure of unparalleled originality* [emphasis mine]. Attempts to maintain the opposite can safely be left to amateur theologians.[38]

This statement includes three assertions. First, Jesus was an actual man, not a fictitious or "mythical" figure. Second, today we know key aspects of Jesus' teaching and conduct by means of historical research. Third, this historical study shows that Jesus of Nazareth was a singular individual. When data about him is laid out, he appears as "a figure of unparalleled originality." While the first and second claims are commonplace, the third is unusual and deserves some consideration.

Kasper reiterates his thesis throughout "The History and Destiny of Jesus Christ." In the one hundred pages that make up this section he refers to Jesus with such phrases as "the category of singularity," "the category of the New," "on the basis of a qualitatively new beginning which is not derivable from history," "a figure of unparalleled originality," "a new, completely fresh start," "a completely new start," "the unprecedented and unparalleled new," and an "initial ignition."[39] Kasper's use of these expressions accentuates his claim: A reconstruction of Jesus' words and deeds reveals that he was a rare sort of man.

This unusual thesis within an historical review prompts three questions. First, why has Kasper made this claim? Second, what kind of logic does he use to argue his case? Third, how successful is this argument?

First, why has Kasper argued for Jesus' "originality"? This is demanded by the post-Enlightenment search for the arrival of a new kind of freedom in history. In this second section of *Jesus the Christ* Kasper is drawing therefore on two distinct sources for Christology. On the one hand, there is the modern commitment to liberation, and, on the other, there is the historical research about Jesus. Working out of these sources, Kasper fashions an historical review aimed at displaying Jesus' singular character. Who was this Jesus? According to Kasper's historical sketch, he was "a qualitatively new beginning which is not derivable from history."

Influenced by the later Schelling, Kasper is convinced that if we are to realize our longing for freedom, we must be helped to do this. Something new must break into our lives, and it must make a difference in our activity. It cannot be some hidden factor, but must be manifest in the give-and-take of human affairs. Of course, not only must this event occur, we must also be able to talk about it. We need a post-Enlightenment view of history that allows for "miraculous" or underivable events. Such an understanding governs Kasper's historical review of Jesus' ministry and death as "the new beginning" in creation.

Second, what kind of logic does Kasper adopt in order to argue this thesis? "The History and Destiny of Jesus Christ" relies on an argument of convergence. In discussing Jesus' conduct, message and death, Kasper highlights historical data and exegetical conclusions in such a way as to show how a number of facts indicate Jesus' character. Kasper does not try to isolate only one specific piece of historical evidence that distinguishes Jesus from all other men and women. Instead, he gathers a wide range of historical material that points to Jesus of Nazareth's unusual stature.

An example of this argument of convergence is the discussion of Jesus' addressing God as Abba. Kasper comments on this usage in his chapter on Jesus' preaching of the kingdom of God. He illuminates some aspects of this message, emphasizing how Jesus refashioned images and concepts of Jewish tradition as well as those of John the Baptist. Then he comments on Jesus' form of address to God:

> The novelty of Jesus' language is that he does not merely describe God as Father as Judaism did, but addresses him as Fa-

ther. The reluctance of Jewish liturgical literature to use this form of address can easily be understood when we know that *abba* is in origin a children's onomatopoeic word (something like 'Daddy'). . . . Calling God *abba* reveals what is new about Jesus' understanding of God: God is close to men in love. The real theological meaning of this use of *abba* appears only when it is seen in connexion with Jesus' message of the kingdom of God.[40]

This statement indicates Kasper's overall argument. Historical data is assembled so that lines of meaning converge. According to Kasper Jesus' proclamation about the kingdom of God exhibits a degree of originality. Jesus has taken familiar views about God's renewal of creation for the chosen people of Israel, and he has shaped these to cast new light on God's compassion and God's proximity to the human family. Simultaneously, Jesus has addressed God by a name rarely ascribed to God by a practicing Jew. He has called God "Daddy," thereby declaring God's intimacy with Jesus and at least indirectly with others. Here are two pieces of information, each of which says something about Jesus. They do not however stand apart in Kasper's presentation. They are discussed side-by-side and then brought together to point toward Jesus' originality.

II.2 *Jesus Is the Kingdom*

Our first two questions about Kasper's post-Enlightenment rationale and his argument of convergence lead to a third: How successful is Kasper's account of Jesus as "a figure of unparalleled originality"? If we assess Kasper's program in terms of an understanding of history in which singular events are in principle impossible, then this endeavor is simply out of bounds. But if we admit the possibility of underivable events, then we can take Kasper's argument seriously. When we do, we find its coherence compelling. Historical data is assembled in such a way that it points to a person, Jesus of Nazareth, who possessed an unusual degree of freedom.

Kasper makes his case by sketching an outline of Jesus' life and reconstructing his preaching, his miracles and death. Then, he reviews early Christian testimony to Jesus' resurrection. In each of these discussions Kasper relates the historical details to Jesus' commitment to the coming of "the kingdom of God." He shows, for instance, how Jesus' cures and exorcisms disclosed the arrival of God's reign within human life.[41] This kind of evidence supports the conclusion that Jesus taught, healed and died with such a radical dedication that he implicitly linked himself with his message: he embodied what he proclaimed, the arrival of God's care in human affairs. Jesus and "the kingdom" are closely connected.

This historical argument is complemented by the discussion of Jesus' freedom. Freedom consists, says Kasper, in the ability to live for God and others.[42] It is characterized by the absence of self-concern, even in the face of death. This kind of detachment can be glimpsed in an historical reconstruction of Jesus' conduct. He announced his message, though questioned by authorities who were concerned about their society's good order. He persisted in proclaiming his message, even when his life was in jeopardy, and he refused to abandon his mission in order to save his life.

There is more to freedom, however, than the ability to act. According to Kasper, liberty exhibits a dialectic of concealment and revelation.[43] Living for others entails the diminishment of self. Jesus' miracles, for instance, do not place Jesus in the spotlight; rather they turn attention to God. Jesus' deeds can be interpreted in different ways. They can be taken, for instance, as expressions of arrogance (Mk 3:21), and hence their significance was discussed by those who knew Jesus. Yet, for Jesus' disciples his wonderful works manifest Jesus as well as God. Concealment and revelation also operate in Jesus' suffering and death and in Jesus' freedom to relinquish control in the face of others' use of their authority.

Kasper's historical review and his comments on freedom converge in his insight that an historical account may both reveal and conceal. Data that to some observers discloses the depth of a person may remain opaque to other observers. As a result, to some people Jesus' suffering and death may indicate his folly, while to others it exhibits his obedience to God. Kasper writes:

> Jesus' death on the cross is the final spelling out of the only
> thing he was interested in, the coming of God's eschatological

rule. This death is the form in which the Kingdom of God exists under the conditions of this age, the Kingdom of God in human powerlessness, wealth in poverty, love in desolation, abundance in emptiness, and life in death.[44]

The idea that freedom allows for both concealment and revelation helps us to understand early Christian testimony to Jesus' resurrection. Nothing in this testimony requires us to believe it. The traditions of the appearances and of the empty tomb do not provide certitude that Jesus was not conquered by death, but overcame death. Hence for some people, who reconstruct the history of Jesus' followers after his death, there is little or nothing here to be discovered. Jesus' group reassembled and founded a sect that happened to flourish. But for others, the historical details about the formation of the first Christian households disclose Jesus' destiny and the arrival of God's reign. Indeed, for those people Jesus' death brought the fullness of life and freedom so that Origen (d. 254) rightly linked Jesus and the kingdom. Alluding to this, Kasper declares that "Jesus is the Kingdom of God in the form of concealment, lowliness and poverty."[45]

The second section of *Jesus the Christ* accomplishes what Kasper intends. It presents Jesus of Nazareth as a man of "unparalleled originality." By uniting historical data about Jesus' ministry and last days with the theme of freedom, Kasper has used an argument of convergence to identify Jesus as a figure of unusual freedom—a freedom that both reveals and conceals his identity. Yet, this presentation would be, I propose, even stronger than it is if its inherent historical narrative about Jesus were made more explicit. To be sure, Kasper has not written a biography about Jesus, but by amassing so many details about Jesus' words, actions and suffering, he has laid out the elements of a drama. This second section, "The History and Destiny of Jesus Christ," conveys an historical narrative about Jesus who lived, preached, and died with a singular freedom, and it would more successfully identify this Jesus if it more deliberately expressed this recital of a person and events. I shall return to this observation after considering the book's third and last section.

III. *Jesus Christ, the Mediator*

The confession "Jesus is the Christ" (Jn 20:31) attests that this Jesus is not only a past figure, but also a living reality today. A Christology of reciprocity considers therefore the risen Christ as well as Jesus of Nazareth, and in *Jesus the Christ* this occurs in section three, "The Mystery of Jesus Christ," where Kasper relies on Scripture and tradition and also on the contemporary thought about freedom. He pursues this investigation under three headings: "Jesus Christ—Son of God," "Jesus Christ—Son of Man," and "Jesus Christ—Mediator between God and Man." Each of these chapters is too complex to be fully reviewed here; therefore I shall simply discuss one key element from each unit.

Who is Jesus Christ? First, he is the Son of God. Jesus is the "Son" who lives in total obedience to the "Father." He receives the fullness of God's love and gives himself completely to God, through the Holy Spirit. Within this dynamism of love, the Son has entered into human affairs and reclaimed them for God. Kasper writes: "The Son is the person who submits himself unreservedly in obedience to God. Thus he is wholly and entirely transparent for God; his obedience is the form in which God is substantially present."[46]

To grasp this view of Christ, I shall make a comparison that Kasper himself does not make. Jesus is like the son who agrees to work in his father's business. He starts out, though, not as the firm's vice-president but as a common laborer. Without privilege, the son works his way up the ladder, and in doing this he comes to understand the business from the bottom up. This humbling experience honors his father, who in founding the business did all of the menial chores. Also, by working from the bottom up, the son rededicates the business to his father. He renews his father's original intention and hence, in a sense, he founds the business anew. In an analogous way, Jesus has given full honor to God by stripping himself of all divine dignity and entering into God's creation as a human being.

In this first perspective, Jesus Christ appears from the outset as one who is intimately united with God. A primary scriptural text in this exercise is Philippians: "Christ Jesus, though he was in the form of God . . . emptied himself, taking the form of a servant. . . . And being found in human form he humbled himself and became obedient unto death, even death on a cross" (Phil 2:6–8). This text, says Kasper, expresses a central insight regarding the reality of God. Jesus' self-denial is nothing less than God's turning to creation in love. God does not coerce creation. God courts us and draws us into the divine life. This idea has been enriched by Hegel and Schelling who in commenting on the vulnerability of love have allowed us to see, says Kasper, that "God's being God must then be conceived as freedom in love which is aware of itself in lavishing itself. . . . [God] *is* in himself the identity and difference between free appeal open to free response and free response open to free acceptance in love."[47] God's total giving and receiving of love has taken place in Jesus Christ, the Son of God.

This first view of Jesus Christ does not however suffice. It needs to be filled out by others. Therefore, we ask again, Who is this Jesus? He is the "son of man," especially in the sense of the "new Adam." He is the one human being who possesses the orientation that God intended for all of creation. Jesus knows his gifts and uses them for the well-being of others and the glory of God. Sustained by the Holy Spirit, he matures to full stature, leads the way for all of creation to realize its potential before God, and becomes the human community's point of union. United with Christ, all people find the source and goal of their lives. As Kasper puts it: "Every man is now defined by the fact that Jesus Christ is his brother, neighbour, comrade, fellow citizen, fellow man."[48]

Let us again work with an image not given by Kasper. Jesus can be compared with a young gymnast. In her training, she not only works on her own skills, but also helps others improve theirs. At the Olympics she performs so superbly that all competitors, despite rivalry and international enmity, are spontaneously moved to applaud her. At the moment of success, she represents the highest aspirations of all athletes. In a similar way, Jesus stands among us as the one whose dedication to God and others enriches our lives and binds us together. Jesus' full humanity is manifest, however, not in a spectacular accomplishment but rather in weakness. Jesus Christ reorientates, "recapitulates," the human community in the concealment of the incarnation, his frustrated ministry, and his suffering and crucifixion. Hidden here is Jesus' redirecting of creation to God—a redirecting that culminates in Jesus' death and resurrection.

In this second perspective, Kasper provides a glimpse of Jesus' bond with humankind. Employing the title the "new Adam," he acknowledges the "solidarity" of all men and women. This bonding oc-

curs through Jesus Christ who stands at the center of life. A primary
scriptural text for Kasper's presentation is Romans 5:12–21: "Then as
one man's trespass led to condemnation for all men, so one man's act of
righteousness leads to acquittal and life for all men" (Rom 5:18). Jesus
Christ is the human family's point of unity who represents all people in
relation to God. He is the basis of true community: "The order of the
universe (peace and reconciliation among men) is possible only if God
himself becomes man, the man for others, and so establishes the beginning of a new human solidarity."[49]

This second view, along with the first, needs to be rounded out with
a third. We ask then for the last time: Who is Jesus Christ? He is "the
mediator between God and man." He is the person in whom God has
become totally united with humankind and in whom humankind has been
brought by the Spirit into full communion with God. At first glance this
union may appear to do violence to God and humankind, for it may appear to violate each party's freedom. But this is not the case. As Kasper
insists:

> [T]he mediation that has occurred in Jesus is not in any way
> in contradiction to man's nature, but is its deepest fulfillment.
> Man as person is, as it were, the indeterminate mediation be-
> tween God and man; in Jesus Christ this receives from God its
> specific form, plenitude and perfection.[50]

This discussion of the union of God and humanity in Jesus Christ
touches on what the Church has spoken of as the "hypostatic union."
To grasp Kasper's understanding of this central doctrine we can again
employ a comparison. Marital love exists in a dialectic of unity and independence.[51] It would appear that the wedding of a man and a woman
would result in the loss of individuality. But there are married couples
who through God's grace and their own efforts live in a relationship that
brings them together and simultaneously sends them out. Each spouse
depends on the other for life, and yet each stands on his or her own. The
bond that has fused their lives has also enabled each of them to tap the
inner resources of their personalities. Thus, from one vantage point who
each of them has become cannot be known apart from the other spouse,
and yet from another vantage point the identity of each is a function of

the unique personality that was emerging in each person before the wedding occurred.

This glimpse of union and individuation in marriage helps us to understand Kasper's presentation on Jesus Christ as God and man.[52] A key scriptural text in this discussion is 1 Timothy 2:5: ''For there is one God, and there is one mediator between God and men, the man Christ Jesus. . . . '' Jesus is the mediator between God and creation. In the person of Jesus Christ, God and humankind are united. We can apprehend what Kasper means here when we recall our remarks above: In the ideal marriage spouses are simultaneously united and individuated. Analogously, Jesus Christ is the true spouse. He lives in perfect union with God, and this union sets him free to live a wholly distinct existence, a human existence. In Chalcedon's terms, Jesus Christ is ''truly God'' and ''truly man.''

Kasper stresses this dialectic of trust and independence. Citing the work of Hegel and Schelling, he expresses the insight that ''the greater the union with God, the greater the intrinsic reality of the man.'' In light of this principle, Jesus Christ is the person who is fully united with God, and thus he is free to become wholly human. To quote Kasper:

> We must say that the indeterminate and open aspect that belongs to the human person is determined definitely by the unity of person with the *Logos,* so that in Jesus through his unity of person with the *Logos,* the human personality comes to its absolutely unique and underivable fulfillment.[53]

This discussion of Jesus Christ as the mediator between God and creation accentuates the theme of freedom that also appears in the other two perspectives on Jesus Christ. In the first view, the Son of God, Jesus, is seen in relation to God: he is God's self-emptying love, and in this he manifests God's freedom to love the other. In the second view, the son of man, Jesus, is perceived in relation to the human community: he is the representative of a renewed human community marked by solidarity, and in this Jesus exhibits the liberating of humankind's freedom to bond with God and creation. In the third view, the mediator, Jesus, the risen Christ, is seen in relation to himself: he is the mediation or perfect relation of God and humankind, united through the Spirit, and in this Jesus Christ realizes in himself the freedom of God and human freedom.

A Christology of reciprocity investigates both the historical Jesus
and the risen Christ. As we previously saw, in his discussion of the historical Jesus, Kasper has drawn on two sources, the post-Enlightenment
notion of freedom and historical research about Jesus. Now we have seen
that in his reflection on the risen Christ, Kasper has brought together the
notion of freedom, on the one hand, and, on the other, Scripture and
tradition. These two sources produce three representations of Jesus
Christ in which the Church's earlier Christological teachings are recast
in the language of emancipation. Jesus Christ is the Savior in the sense
that he is the liberator of humankind. He has freed the human family
from disobedience and death, and he has led it to fidelity to God and thus
to the fullness of life. As a result, in *Jesus the Christ* the presentation on
the risen Christ complements the earlier account of the historical Jesus.
Together the two sections provide what the reciprocal method aims at: a
balanced inquiry into the contemporary meaning of the ancient confession that Jesus is the Christ.

IV.1 *A Reciprocal Method: An Appraisal*

Jesus the Christ represents what Kasper calls "a Christology of reciprocity," "a Christology of complementarity." It is not limited to one
source, but makes use of at least three sources, the Church today, history, and Scripture and tradition. In this reliance on different wellsprings, it attempts to focus simultaneously on, to "reciprocate" between, the historical Jesus and the risen Christ, as though linking the two
foci of an ellipse. Having analyzed Kasper's use of this reciprocal
method, we can locate it in relation to other theological methods, and
then we can assess it, especially as adopted by Kasper.

One way of classifying today's various theological methods distinguishes between Christology "from above" and Christology "from
below." This distinction is however problematic, for its metaphors can
be understood in various senses.[54] For example, "from below" can
describe a Christology like Rahner's that begins with a general understanding of personal existence, or it can fit a Christology like Schillebeeckx's that starts with an historical reconstruction of Jesus'
ministry. The scheme of "from above"/"from below" is at best a
modest instrument which, when applied to *Jesus the Christ,* points out

that this book incorporates both strategies for knowing Jesus Christ.[55] It begins "from below" in that it relies on an historical review of Jesus' teaching, activities and last days, and at the same time it starts "from above" in that it reflects on Scripture's and tradition's claims about the exalted Lord.

Another way to place this reciprocal method is to locate it within the heritage of the Catholic Tübingen School.[56] The Catholic faculty of theology at the University of Tübingen dates to 1817, when the Catholic instructors at Ellwangen, midway between Stuttgart and Nuremburg, moved to Tübingen, south of Stuttgart, to share facilities with the university's long established Protestant faculty. Since its inception, the Catholic faculty has possessed therefore an ecumenical thrust. Moreover, it has also aimed at integrating the retrieval of the Christian tradition, the critical study of history, and the adoption of modern thought. This ambitious agenda has been pursued by its renowned theologians, including J. D. von Drey (d. 1853), J. A. Möhler (d. 1836), J. E. Kuhn (d. 1887), F. A. Staudenmaier (d. 1856), K. Adam (d. 1966), and J. R. Geiselmann (d. 1970). Having studied at Tübingen and taught there since 1974, as the Catholic faculty's professor of dogmatic theology, Kasper deliberately stands within this heritage's commitment to a theological synthesis, manifest in a Christology of reciprocity.[57]

Finally, there is yet another way of classifying the theological method of *Jesus the Christ*. Avery Dulles has described Kasper's theology as "kerygmatic and dogmatic."[58] That is, his Christology commences, as we have seen, with the early confession "Jesus is the Christ," and then it unfolds as it mines the riches of the Church's creeds and teachings. Kasper himself notes that his method bears a family resemblance to that of his Tübingen predecessors Adam and Geiselmann who recognized that Jesus Christ is "accessible only through biblical and ecclesiastical tradition."[59] Further, this approach has much in common with the convictions and aims of the great Protestant theologian Karl Barth whose work has been characterized by Kasper as an "ecclesial-dogmatic Christology."[60]

The validity of Kasper's method of reciprocity is grounded in its breadth. Its acknowledgment of three sources for Christology yields a many-faceted view of Christ. He is the historical Jesus, the doctrinal

Christ, and the liberating Lord. This inclusivity makes *Jesus the Christ* an appealing text. In fact, it has been widely adopted in colleges and seminaries, says Brian McDermott, "because of its contemporaneity, responsibility to the tradition, and attention to exegetical and historical data."[61] Aidan Nichols makes a similar observation when he points out that Kasper's work offers "a *via media* or *re-accentramento* ('re-centring') for Church and theology, amid the competing voices of left and right-wing radicalism in post-conciliar Catholicism."[62]

Jesus the Christ does however manifest two possible shortcomings of its synthetic approach. First, the results of exegetical and historical study appear at times to be forced to align with tradition. For example, Kasper declares that Jesus suffered more than any other human being.[63] Also, he maintains that Jesus viewed his death as salvific.[64] Both of these claims rest more upon post-Easter witness than upon the consensus of modern historians and exegetes.[65] Though it need not happen, a reciprocal method can ask too much from historical and exegetical research.

A second possible shortcoming of a method of this sort is that one linguistic form can overwhelm other forms of discourse about Jesus Christ. A synthesis of such diverse, rich sources risks giving priority to the terminology of one source over the others. Given our age's preference for discursive or conceptual talk, narratives and figuration can be neglected. One symptom of this in *Jesus the Christ* is the density of some portions of the text. In section two the meaning of "new beginning" and "underivable event" is not always clear, and in section three discussions about freedom are at points difficult to follow. Philosophical talk about liberation overshadows at times more narrative ways of expressing what "freedom" means.

These two possible shortcomings can be remedied. First, historical data need not be presented as an apologetic for Christian faith. It suffices to demonstrate that the findings of exegetes and historians do not detract from the insights attained by the Christian community over the centuries. Second, the predominance of one form of language can be resolved through a more deliberate recognition that Christology relies on figurative discourse as well as on more theoretical language. I shall conclude this chapter by calling attention to these implicit narratives and their function in *Jesus the Christ*.

IV.2 *Narratives and Christology*

Identifying another person, as outlined in Chapter One, entails the use of names and titles, physical description, and biography. At first glance, there may appear to be little resemblance between this and the approach to the identity of Jesus Christ displayed in *Jesus the Christ.* Ordinarily one source, biography, enables us to express who someone is. In the case of Jesus Christ, three sources are required: the contemporary Church's experience, historical research, and Scripture and tradition. Our knowledge of Jesus Christ can seem to depend therefore on a process unlike our familiar ways of knowing another person. On closer inspection however we can discern that the reciprocal method as found in *Jesus the Christ* is comparable to our ordinary ways of saying who someone is. In light of this, we can see how Christology can be enriched by a more explicit use of narratives.

Forms of narrative are implicit in *Jesus the Christ,* specifically in both the second section, "The History and Destiny of Jesus Christ," and the third, "The Mystery of Jesus." Kasper's historical review of Jesus' ministry and last days conveys a narrative. As we have already noted, Kasper marshals historical data within an argument of convergence. This does not produce a biography of Jesus. Yet, this assembling of material about a life conveys an historical narrative about Jesus. In his comments on theological method, Kasper acknowledges that historical reconstruction yields an implicit narrative when he states that Christology "has to narrate a real and actual story—history—and to bear testimony to it."[66] Such a narrative runs through "The History and Destiny of Jesus Christ."

Kasper's consideration of Scripture and tradition is also shaped by narratives—not historical narratives, but biblical stories. Each of the three views of Jesus Christ alludes to a story. The presentation on the Son of God tells of one who relinquished his stature as God and became a slave (Phil 2).[67] The account of the new Adam recalls one who disobeyed God's rule, thereby fracturing the harmony of the human family. But he was eventually followed by another whose life of obedience unto death restored faithfulness to God and neighbor (Rom 5).[68] Finally, the discussion of the mediator tells of one who lived within the world, proclaimed God's word among the peoples, and was drawn into God's glory (1 Tim 3).[69] While these recollections cannot be classified as either histories or biographies, they are forms of narrative. They recount a sequence of "events" in which a main character, Jesus Christ, is depicted as he acts and suffers.

In noting the implicit narratives in *Jesus the Christ,* I am making more than a rhetorical or stylistic point. Narratives influence the meaning of words in many ways, and two such ways are pertinent here. First, as we saw in Chapter One, in ordinary discourse biography shapes the meaning of a person's titles. While to some extent a title is defined by social conventions, at a certain point what a title means is determined by the behavior of the person who holds the title. For example, "president" depends on the office as described in an organization's laws, but it is also a function of the conduct of the office-holder. Since this conduct is recounted in anecdotes and biography, these serve as rules of speech.

This logic extends to Christology in that scriptural narratives determine the meaning of the titles we ascribe to Jesus. For instance, when Christians call Jesus the Son of God, they use this title in ways governed by scriptural stories. This point has been made by Terrence Tilley in *Story Theology.* In Tilley's words: "To understand these titles [of Jesus] requires understanding the stories in which they were set, the uses which the New Testament writers made of those metaphors and stories, and the significance they have in the canonical Scriptures."[70] In support of this claim, Tilley has shown how such titles as "Son of God," "son of man," and "new Adam" are defined by narratives from the Bible. These are the very texts upon which Kasper has relied in *Jesus the Christ.* In other words, Tilley has confirmed that narratives form the kind of inquiry Kasper has undertaken in his third section, "The Mystery of Jesus."

Second, biography specifies the meaning of our words for human traits and aspirations. What we mean when we say that someone is good or holy or compassionate depends in part on the accompanying narratives. In a similar way, we rely on concrete instances to display the specific meaning of our ideals, for example, "freedom," "justice," "peace," and "love." By recollecting instances of these ideals as lived out, we show what they signify. David Burrell has clarified that some analogous terms receive their exact meaning from the narratives with which they are associated. Regarding for example the word "loving," Burrell states:

Any attempt to define *loving* will itself involve ambiguous terms, and these will require to be elucidated in turn by salient examples. This semantic fact clinches the case: it is not simply that we may be unable to find an unambiguous formula for *loving,* but that it is impossible to find one. So recourse to narrative illustration is not a *faute de mieux;* there simply is no better way.[71]

This logic also obtains when we use these terms in our talk about God and Jesus Christ. As Burrell has shown, religious discourse puts some words to new uses by trading on the openness of their meaning.[72] Attribute terms (e.g., "good" and "merciful") and aspiration terms (e.g., "love" and "freedom") function well in talk about God and Christ because they receive their exact meaning from the narratives and images with which they are linked. To understand what these words mean in a given account we need to refer to the narratives that stand as their linguistic rules. Thus, for example, to grasp what Kasper means by the freedom of Jesus Christ, we need to be aware of the primary scriptural stories in "The Mystery of God."

Earlier I observed that one of the shortcomings of *Jesus the Christ* is its density. While part of this may be attributed to Kasper's admirable feat of keeping the text to approximately two hundred and seventy-five pages, part of the difficulty may further stem from the lack of narration within the text. The use of "new beginning" and "underivable event" in section two, "The History and Destiny of Jesus," would be clearer if Kasper's historical narrative about Jesus were more explicit. Also, the meaning of the titles and the notion of freedom in section three, "The Mystery of Jesus," would be more intelligible, if the respective scriptural narratives were retold.

In my review of section three, I have sought to draw out the implicit narratives by the use of comparable narratives: the son who works in his father's firm, the internationally acclaimed gymnast, and the perfect spouse. These images allude to the metaphors at the heart of Kasper's presentation. Without them, it is hard to explain the text. With them, light is shed on the biblical stories that implicitly contribute to Kasper's overall argument.

At this point, one might well ask what a Christology would look like if its narratives were more on the surface. One example of what I have in mind occurs in the writings of Karl Barth.[73] Narratives play an explicit role in Barth's Christology. In the fourth volume of the *Church Dogmatics* Barth retells biblical stories.[74] For example, he recounts the drama running through the Synoptic Gospels. Moreover, Barth specifies his narrative motifs by using figurative titles in the *Church Dogmatics,* volume IV: "The Way of the Son of God into the Far Country" (Vol. IV/1), "The Homecoming of the Son of Man" (Vol. IV/2), and "The Glory of the Mediator" (Vol. IV/3,1). Each of these titles alludes to a familiar image: traveling abroad, returning home, and receiving an honor.

Interestingly, Barth's *Church Dogmatics,* IV, and Kasper's *Jesus the Christ* follow a similar threefold pattern.[75] First, Jesus is seen as the Son of God, second, as the son of man, and, third, as the mediator between God and humankind. This is not accidental, for in "The Mystery of God" Kasper often refers to Barth's work. This resemblance between the two texts suggests that the ways Barth has employed biblical narratives would also benefit Kasper's work. There is however a notable qualification. Whereas Barth accentuates one source for Christology, namely the Bible, Kasper relies on three sources: the Church today, historical research, and Scripture and tradition. In light of this difference, I propose that Kasper's reciprocal Christology be enlarged through explicit adoption of diverse kinds of narratives.

My proposal is threefold. First, since one source of Christology is historical research, I propose that we include a loose form of a biography of Jesus within systematic inquiry. In other words, we fashion historical reconstruction into an historical narrative. An example of this is found in Edward Schillebeeckx's *Jesus.* Second, another source is tradition, and, in order to respect the reliance of Scripture and tradition on the category of narrative, I propose that we incorporate the retelling of a Gospel or Gospels into Christology. That is, we regard the Gospels as stories that must be read on their own terms. An instance of this occurs in Frans Jozef van Beeck's *Christ Proclaimed.* Third, since a source of Christology is today's Church, I propose that we draw on a modern saint's witness to the living Christ. Hence, within Christology we can recount the life of an exemplary Christian disciple, for example, that of Dorothy Day. In sum, here are three distinct kinds of narratives that can be explicitly incorporated into a Christology of complementarity.

Jesus the Christ displays a paradigm of how we can identify the one whom Christians acclaim as Lord. On the one hand, this process is unusual, for it depends on three sources, and normally when we say who someone is, we rely on a single source, biography. On the other hand, narratives are at work in Kasper's Christology, and this means that our identifying of Jesus Christ is analogous to our more familiar endeavor of telling someone's biography. Therefore, Christology can take some of its bearings from our ordinary discourse. In the next three chapters I shall attempt to do this, with the help of Schillebeeckx's *Jesus* and van Beeck's *Christ Proclaimed*. The aim here is to enrich a reciprocal method in Christology. In so doing, we shall be better equipped to identify the person who, as Brother Roger Schutz says, "suffers with all who suffer" and "rejoices with all who rejoice."

NOTES

1. Brother Roger Schutz, Interview, *America,* CLII (January 22, 1983), p. 50. Cf. Mother Teresa of Calcutta and Brother Roger of Taizé, *Meditations on the Way of the Cross* (New York: The Pilgrim Press, 1987).

2. Walter Kasper, *Jesus the Christ,* trans. by V. Green (New York: Paulist, 1976), p. 15.

3. Walter Kasper, *The God of Jesus Christ,* trans. M.J. O'Connell (New York: Crossroad, 1984); *idem,* "Die Kirche als universales Sakrament des Heils," in: Elmar Klinger and Klaus Wittstadt (eds.), *Glaube im Prozess* (Herder: Freiburg, 1984), pp. 221–239. Cf. The German Bishops' Conference, *Katholischer Erwachsenen Katechismus* (Stuttgart: Verlag Katholisches Bibelwerk, 1985).

4. Walter Kasper, "The Spirit Acting in the World To Demolish Frontiers and Create the Future," *Lumen Vitae,* XXXIV (1979), 86–99; *idem,* "Aspekts gegenwärtiger Pneumatologie," in: *idem, Gegenwart des Geistes* (Freiburg: Herder, 1979), 7–22.

5. Walter Kasper, "Hope in the Final Coming of Jesus Christ in Glory," *Communio,* XII (1985), 368–384; *idem,* "Christologie und Anthropologie," *Theologische Quartalschrift,* CLII (1982), 202–221.

6. Book reviews of *Jesus the Christ* include: Gerard S. Sloyan, *Commonweal,* CV (April 14, 1978), 251–254; Aloys Grillmeier, *Theologie und Philosophie,* LI (1976), 254–257; Karl Neufeld, "Zu: Walter Kasper, Jesus der Christus," *Zeitschrift für katholische Theologie,* XCVIII (1976), 180–185 [with response by Kasper, pp. 186–189]; Walter Kern, *Stimmen der Zeit,* CXCIII (1975), 516–528; Bruce Vawter, *Theological Studies,* XXXVI (1975), 772–774.

7. Kasper, *Jesus the Christ*, p. 230.

8. *Ibid.*, pp. 41–61. Cf. Walter Kasper, *An Introduction to the Christian Faith*, trans. by V. Green (New York: Paulist, 1980), pp. 1–18; *idem*, "Autonomie und Theonomie," in: Helmut Weber and Dietmar Mieth (eds.), *Anspruch der Wirklichkeit und Christlicher Glaube* (Düsseldorf: Patmos Verlag, 1980), pp. 17–41.

9. Kasper, *Jesus the Christ*, pp. 37–38.

10. Appraisals of Kasper's Christology include: Aidan Nichols, "Walter Kasper and His Theological Programme," *New Blackfriars*, LXVII (January, 1986), 16–24; Brian O. McDermott, "Roman Catholic Christology," *Theological Studies*, XLI (1980), 339–367; William Loewe, "The New Catholic Tübingen Theology of Walter Kasper," *The Heythrop Journal*, XXI (1980), 30–49; Thomas McFadden, "Christology," in: *The New Catholic Encyclopedia*, XVII (Washington, D.C.: McGraw-Hill, 1979), pp. 113–116; Dietrich Wiederkehr, "Christologie im Kontext," in: Josef Pfammatter (ed.), *Theologische Berichte* 7 (Zurich: Benziger, 1978), pp. 56–62; Philip Rosato, "Spirit Christology," *Theological Studies*, XXXVIII (1977), 423–449.

11. Kasper, *Jesus the Christ*, pp. 26–40; *idem*, "Neuansätze gegenwärtiger Christologie," in: *idem* (ed.), *Christologische Schwerpunkte* (Düsseldorf: Patmos, 1980), pp. 17–36. Cf. David Tracy, *The Analogical Imagination* (New York: Crossroad Publishers, 1981), p. 335 n. 21.

12. Kasper has recognized the importance of narratives in theology; cf. W. Kasper, "Systematisch-theologische Neuansätze," *Theologische Quartalschrift*, CLVI (1979), 55–61. Others have also suggested that greater use could be made of the figurative elements in Kasper's Christology; cf. Loewe, "The New Catholic Tübingen Theology of Walter Kasper," pp. 45–49; Nicholas Lash, *Theology on Dover Beach* (New York: Paulist Press, 1979), p. 174.

13. Kasper, *Jesus the Christ*, p. 19; cf. *idem*, "Die Sache Jesu," *Herder Korrespondenz*, XXVI (1972), 185–189; *idem*, "Christologie von unten? Kritik und Neuansatz gegenwärtiger Christologie," in: Leo Scheffczyk (ed.), *Grundfragen der Christologie heute* (Freiburg: Herder, 1975), pp. 141–183 [including a response by H. Küng].

14. Kasper, *Jesus the Christ*, pp. 48–51; cf. *idem*, "Karl Rahner—Theologe in einer Zeit des Umbruchs," *Theologische Quartalschrift*, CLIX (1979), 263–271.

15. Kasper, *Jesus the Christ*, pp. 15, 24, 163; cf. *idem*, "Aufgabe der Christologie heute," in: Arno Schilson and W. Kasper (eds.), *Christologie im Praesens* (Freiburg: Herder, 1974), pp. 133–151.

16. Kasper, *Jesus the Christ*, p. 37.

17. *Ibid.*, p. 35. This is the background to Kasper's critique of Edward

Schillebeeckx's *Jesus;* cf. Walter Kasper, "Liberale Christologie," *Evangelischer Kommentar*, VI (1976), 357–360.

18. Kasper, *Jesus the Christ*, p. 26.

19. *Ibid.*, p. 27.

20. *Ibid.*, pp. 30, 61 n. 53, 246; cf. *idem*, "Christologie und Anthropologie," p. 210 n. 34.

21. Kasper, *Jesus the Christ*, p. 55; *idem*, "Anthropologische Aspekte der Busse," *Theologische Quartalschrift*, CLXIII (1983), 102–103; *idem*, "The Theological Problem of Evil," in: W. Kasper, *Faith and the Future*, trans. R. Nowell (New York: Crossroad Publishing, 1982), pp. 109–133.

22. On Schelling's Christology, see: Thomas F. O'Meara, "Christ in Schelling's *Philosophy of Revelation*," *The Heythrop Journal*, XXVII (1986), 275–289; *idem*, *Romantic Idealism and Roman Catholicism* (Notre Dame: University of Notre Dame Press, 1982). On Hegel's Christology, see: E. Brito, *La Christologie de Hegel* (Paris: Beauchesne, 1983); J. Yerkes, *The Christology of Hegel* (Albany: SUNY Press, 1983).

23. Kasper, *Jesus the Christ*, pp. 47–48, 54–58; cf. Kasper's "Habilitationsschrift": *Das Absolute in der Geschichte: Philosophie und Theologie der Geschichte in der Spatphilosophie Schellings* (Mainz: Matthias Grünewald, 1965). On Kasper's reliance on Schelling's thought, see Loewe, "The New Catholic Tübingen Theology of Walter Kasper."

24. Kasper, *Jesus the Christ*, pp. 47, 56. On the Frankfurt School, see: Rudolf A. Siebert, *The Critical Theory of Religion* (New York: Walter de Gruyter, 1983); Francis Schüssler Fiorenza, "Critical Social Theory and Christology," *Proceedings of the Catholic Theological Society*, XXX (1975), pp. 63–110; Martin Jay, *The Dialectical Imagination* (Boston: Little, Brown and Company, 1973).

25. Kasper, *Jesus the Christ*, p. 191; cf. *idem*, *Glaube im Wandel der Geschichte* (Mainz: Matthias Grünewald Verlag, 1970).

26. Cf. Walter Kasper, "Krise und Neuanfang der Christologie im Denken Schellings," *Evangelische Theologie*, XXXIII (1973), 366–384.

27. Walter Kasper, "Dogmatik als Wissenschaft," *Theologische Quartalschrift*, CLVII (1977), 189–203; *idem*, "Tradition als Erkenntnisprinzip," *Theologische Quartalschrift*, CLV (1975), 198–215; *idem*, *Dogma unter dem Wort Gottes* (Mainz: Matthias Grünewald Verlag, 1965).

28. Kasper, *Jesus the Christ*, pp. 35–36.

29. Walter Kasper, *The Methods of Dogmatic Theology*, trans. by J. Drury (Dublin: Ecclesia, 1969), p. 7.

30. Kasper, *Jesus the Christ*, p. 28.

31. *Ibid.*, p. 42.

32. Walter Kasper, "Einmaligkeit und Universalität," *Theologie der Gegenwart*, XVII (1974), 1–11.

33. Alister E. McGrath, *The Making of Modern German Christology* (New York: Basil Blackwell, 1986), pp. 9–31.

34. Kasper, *Jesus the Christ*, p. 42.

35. *Ibid.*, pp. 15, 35.

36. *Ibid.*, p. 20.

37. *Ibid.*, p. 35.

38. *Ibid.*, p. 65.

39. *Ibid.*, pp. 65–162 *passim.*

40. *Ibid.*, p. 80.

41. *Ibid.*, p. 98.

42. *Ibid.*, pp. 54–55.

43. *Ibid.*, p. 97.

44. *Ibid.*, p. 119.

45. *Ibid.*, p. 100.

46. *Ibid.*, p. 166.

47. *Ibid.*, p. 183.

48. *Ibid.*, p. 205.

49. *Ibid.*, p. 225.

50. *Ibid.*, p. 247.

51. Cf. Walter Kasper, *Theology of Christian Marriage*, trans. D. Smith (New York: The Crossroad Publishing Company, 1983).

52. Kasper, *Jesus the Christ*, pp. 230–252.

53. *Ibid.*, p. 248.

54. On the distinction between "from above"/"from below," see: Nicholas Lash, "Up and Down in Christology," in: Stephen Sykes and J.D. Holmes (eds.), *New Studies in Theology, I* (London: SCM Press, 1976); Hans Georg Koch, "Neue Wege in der Christologie," *Herder Korrespondenz*, XXIX (1975), 412–418; Peter C. Hodgson, *Jesus—Word and Presence* (Philadelphia: Fortress Press, 1971), pp. 60–65. ,

55. Kasper, *Jesus the Christ*, pp. 36–38, 166; *idem*, "Neuansätze gegenwärtiger Christologie," pp. 17–20; *idem*, "Christologie von unten? Kritik und Neuansatz gegenwärtiger Christologie," in: Scheffczyk (ed.), *Grundfragen der Christologie heute*, pp. 141–183.

56. On the Catholic Tübingen School, see: Wayne Fehr, *The Birth of the Tübingen School* (Chico: Scholars Press, 1981); James Burtchaell, "Drey, Möhler and the Catholic School of Tübingen," in: Ninian Smart *et al.* (eds.), *Nineteenth Century Religious Thought in the West* (Cambridge: Cambridge University Press, 1985), pp. 111–139; *idem, Catholic Theories of Biblical Inspiration Since 1810* (Cambridge: Cambridge University Press, 1969), pp. 1–

43; O'Meara, *Romantic Idealism and Roman Catholicism, passim;* Gerald A. McCool, *Catholic Theology in the Nineteenth Century* (New York: Seabury, 1977), *passim;* Elmar Klinger, "Tübingen School," in: Karl Rahner *et al.* (eds.), *Sacramentum Mundi,* VI (New York: Herder, 1970), pp. 318–320.

57. Cf. Walter Kasper, "Verständnis der Theologie Damals und Heute," in: J. Ratzinger and J. Newmann (eds.), *Theologie im Wandel,* I (Munich: Erich Wewel, 1967), pp. 90–115.

58. Avery Dulles, "Contemporary Approaches to Christology," *The Living Light,* XIII (1976), 119–144.

59. Kasper, *Jesus the Christ,* p. 9.

60. *Ibid.,* p. 32.

61. McDermott, "Roman Catholic Christology," p. 339.

62. Nichols, "Walter Kasper and His Theological Programme," p. 16.

63. Kasper, *Jesus the Christ,* p. 118.

64. *Ibid.,* p. 220.

65. Cf. Gerald O'Collins, *What Are They Saying About Jesus?,* Second Edition (New York: Paulist, 1977), *passim;* John P. Galvin, "The Resurrection in Catholic Systematics," *The Heythrop Journal,* XX (1979), 130–132; *idem,* "Jesus' Approach to Death," *Theological Studies,* XL (1980), pp. 732–734.

66. Kasper, *Jesus the Christ,* p. 20.

67. *Ibid.,* p. 168.

68. *Ibid.,* p. 205; cf. 197.

69. *Ibid.,* p. 231.

70. Terrence Tilley, *Story Theology* (Wilmington: Michael Glazier, 1985), p. 117.

71. David B. Burrell, "Argument in Theology," in: Carl Raschke (ed.), *New Dimensions in Philosophical Theology* (Chico: Scholars Press, 1982), pp. 37–51, 46.

72. Cf. David Burrell, *Analogy and Philosophical Language* (New Haven: Yale University Press, 1974), pp. 226–230; *idem, Aquinas: God and Action* (Notre Dame: University of Notre Dame Press, 1979).

73. On Barth's use of biblical narrative, see: David H. Kelsey, *The Uses of Scripture in Recent Theology* (Philadelphia: Fortress, 1975), pp. 32–55; David F. Ford, "Barth's Interpretation of the Bible," in: S.W. Sykes (ed.), *Karl Barth* (Oxford: Clarendon, 1979), pp. 55–87; James Coughenour, "Karl Barth and the Gospel Story," *Andover Newton Quarterly,* XX (1979), 97–110.

74. Cf. Karl Barth, *Church Dogmatics,* edited by G.W. Bromiley and T.E. Torrance (Edinburgh: T.&T. Clark, 1953-1959), IV/1–3.

75. For Kasper's references to Barth's work, see: Kasper, *Jesus the Christ,* pp. 32, 36, 40 n. 52, 183, 195 n. 46, 195 n. 52, p. 254, p. 272 n. 75.

Chapter Three

A BIOGRAPHY OF JESUS?

A biography of Jesus is not currently possible. The historical data is simply lacking. Nevertheless, in recent years historians and exegetes have reached a consensus about some important details in Jesus' life and times, so that we can now assemble more than an odd assortment of facts about Jesus. Today it is possible to recollect aspects of the Nazarean's ministry and last days. That is, we can fashion an account that is on the one hand more than an historical reconstruction and on the other less than a biography. In a word, we can construct an historical narrative about Jesus.

This proposal immediately prompts questions of feasibility and significance.[1] First, what would such an historical narrative look like, and would it hold up under historians' and exegetes' critical eye? Second, what would this kind of account contribute to a systematic inquiry that historical reconstruction does not already provide? What is the theological significance of ordering the historical material within a narrative?

Both sorts of questions will be pursued in this third chapter. As the first step, they can be answered now in a tentative way. An historical narrative about Jesus begins with Jesus' baptism by John the Baptist, reviews his teaching, recounts some of Jesus' activities, tells of his last days in Jerusalem, and ends with the reassembling of Jesus' followers. What does this account add to Christology? The sequential shape of this account is valuable because it produces fresh historical images of Jesus that are distinct from—though possibly complementary to—biblical images of Jesus. By linking in a single drama some of Jesus' words and deeds, an historical narrative more fully identifies the Nazarean than does an historical reconstruction. As a result, it stands as a stronger independent point of reference beside the testimonies of tradition and today's Church. The thesis of this third chapter is therefore that historical narratives are one important source for Christology.

Edward Schillebeeckx is a major proponent of Christology's reliance on historical narratives about Jesus.[2] He has argued for this in his *Jesus: An Experiment in Christology* which appeared in 1974 (the same year as Walter Kasper's *Jesus the Christ* and Hans Küng's *On Being a Christian*).[3] This book's second part, "The Gospel of Jesus Christ," consists of an account in which the author arranges historical and exegetical material within a drama whose major character is Jesus, "the latter-day prophet."[4] This "post-critical narrative history" and its role within Schillebeeckx's systematic inquiry provides one response to the questions I have posed above, and thus it can serve as the case study for my proposal about Christology's explicit reliance on historical narratives.

My turning to *Jesus* for guidance may appear odd. Shortly after its publication, this text was reviewed by Kasper who has located it within the heritage of "liberal theology," especially similar to the work of Wilhelm Hermann (d. 1922).[5] According to Kasper, *Jesus* is a one-sided Christology because it draws primarily on one source, historical study, and neglects another, tradition. This assessment was challenged by Schillebeeckx in his *Interim Report*. He noted, first, that Kasper had not grasped some aspects of the book because he inappropriately tied it to a debate then current in Tübingen, and, second, that while Kasper's Christology and Schillebeeckx's differ, "[b]oth perspectives are legitimate."[6] In light of this exchange, I wish to clarify that I do not intend to adjudicate the differences between these two reputable theologians.

I want to develop further the theological approach exhibited in *Jesus the Christ*. This reciprocal method stands in sharp contrast to the "historical and genetic" method of *Jesus*.[7] Whereas Kasper regards history as one source among others, Schillebeeckx considers history as the main source and starting point for his "experiment." The two theologians have pursued different aims in their books, and they have accomplished these by means of their distinct methods. I do not intend to combine their respective approaches, nor to measure one against the other.

My goal is to show that the second major section of *Jesus the Christ* would be enriched if its underlying narrative were made explicit like the one expressed in the second part of *Jesus*. Kasper's historical reconstruction in his "History and Destiny of Jesus Christ" and Schillebeeckx's historical review in his "The Gospel of Jesus Christ" bear a family resemblance. Both are forms of Christology "from below." One formal way in which they differ, however, is that Schillebeeckx's narrative is evident, while Kasper's is not. So that one element in Kasper's reciprocal method can benefit from one aspect of Schillebeeckx's historical and genetic approach, I shall pursue three questions. First, what is the literary form of Schillebeeckx's account of Jesus' ministry and death? Second, how does this function within *Jesus?* Third, what would such an account contribute to a reciprocal method in Christology?

I.1 *"A Post-Critical Narrative History"*

In the mid-1700's, Herman Reimarus (d. 1768) pioneered what today is a generally accepted idea: the Gospels are not histories in the modern sense.[8] Matthew, Mark, Luke and John did not write biographies of Jesus. Further, after Reimarus, one attempt after another failed to construct a valid biography of Jesus, and this led to Albert Schweitzer's (d. 1965) brilliant demonstration in *The Quest of the Historical Jesus* (1906) that we cannot dig out the historical Jesus from the Scriptures. The one hundred and fifty years from Reimarus through Schweitzer have set key limits for late twentieth century queries about the historical Jesus. Yet, in recent years this discussion has entered a new phase.

A post-critical view of Jesus is now possible, insists Schillebeeckx, with a hand on the work of Paul Ricoeur. While biblical writers manifest the ancient world's "narrative innocence," we have reached the point at which we can consciously adopt a "second innocence."[9] Standing on the other side of the Enlightenment, we can maintain a critical distance from the testimonies we receive, and simultaneously we can now recount the events behind these testimonies in such a way that we express the ways these events are linked. We can move beyond an historical analysis to an historical synthesis—a synthesis which reflects the role of imagination in human cognition. This concretely means that without forfeiting our critical skills we can assemble historical data about Jesus in order to fashion "a post-critical narrative history."

This kind of narrative has been presented in the second part of *Jesus.* Entitled "The Gospel of Jesus Christ," it extends approximately three hundred pages.[10] As commentators have pointed out, Schillebeeckx's account is a tour de force in historical research and biblical exegesis. This "history" consists of four parts: (1) Jesus' "message," (2) Jesus' "manner of life," (3) Jesus' "rejection and death," and (4) the disciples after Jesus' death. A brief summary of this impressive study exhibits that it is indeed an historical narrative, a recital of events in Jesus' ministry.

Jesus' Message

Jesus heard John's preaching and was baptized by John in the Jordan. This was a "disclosure experience" for Jesus. The times were colored by premonitions of the end of the world. With his stark appearance and stern call to repentance, John the Baptizer drew a sizable following of Palestinian Jews. He forcefully reiterated Deutero-Isaiah's message of God's impending judgment upon humankind (Is 40:3). Eventually, though, John failed; he was beheaded by Herod Antipas (Mk 6:7).

Jesus adopted John's message of *metanoia*, though he added a new emphasis by stressing God's care and forgiveness. Whereas John was the "prophet of woe," Jesus was "the prophet of salvation." John lived apart. Jesus ate with Pharisees, fishermen, prostitutes and tax collectors (Mk 2:16). Like John, Jesus declared the imminent arrival of God's kingdom. Unlike John, Jesus spoke of God's offer of compassion—an offer being made in the present and to be fully realized in the future.

The parables and the beatitudes convey Jesus' message. The parables' use of paradox and their everyday subject matter announce that God is among us in ways we least expect. God is the almighty One (Lk 12:20; 17:7-10) who is generous (Lk 18:10-14) and magnanimous (Mt 18:23ff). The advent of God's rule demands watchfulness (Mt 24:45-51). The parable of the unimportant slave (Lk 17:7-10) sets the Jewish law in relation to God. What God's rule asks is not juridical observance of the law, but complete dedication to God: "We are unworthy servants; we have only done what was our duty" (Lk 17:10). In the parable of the unmerciful servant (Mt 18:23-25) one slave, having had his debt remitted by his master, refuses to have mercy on a fellow slave, and for this lack of mercy he is punished by the master. God's lordship is one of forgiveness, before which some people repent and forgive their neighbors.

Jesus' Conduct

Jesus' actions confirm his words. His miracles show God's care, as when he heals Peter's mother-in-law (Mk 1:30-31). God's saving invitation is revealed in Jesus' offer of companionship. He draws an odd assortment of people to his table. For example, he dines with Pharisees and adulterers (Lk 7:36-50), tax collectors and faithful followers (Mk 2:15-17). In his company people share the little they have so that it multiplies (Mk 6:34-44). Also, Jesus beckons people to be his co-workers in spreading the "good news" (Mk 6:7-13). In his miracles and companionship, Jesus brings about God's new rule, and, as a result, he is seen by many as the prophet of the last days (Dt 18:15–18).

Jesus redefined a Jew's relationship to the Jewish structures. He acted as the "liberator from a constricting view of God." On occasion he broke the sabbath's fast, thereby declaring the relativity of the law. Simultaneously, Jesus gave a radical rendering of the law, as is evident in his pronouncement on divorce (Mt 5:32). This is also clear in his prophetic gesture of "cleansing" the temple's courtyard (Mt 11:15–18)— a gesture symbolizing Israel's need for conversion and setting the law in relation to a higher standard, God. Eventually Jesus was arrested for "disturbing the peace."

Jesus' use of Abba in his personal prayer is striking.[11] It separates Jesus from most of his contemporaries. This practice indicates Jesus' sense of his close relationship with God, and it gives a clue to the source of Jesus' behavior. In the last analysis, the locus of Jesus' authority is not the law but his filial experience of God.

Jesus' Rejection and Death

Jesus was not surprised by his arrest.[12] He had intimations of his fate since his "fiasco in Galilee." In the hill country Jesus experienced the rejection of his message (Mk 7; Lk 7:18-23), and he must have felt that he too was rejected by the people at large. This failure led him to select an inner circle of twelve to carry on his work. By the time he went "up to Jerusalem," he knew that this would put his life in jeopardy. Nevertheless, he had to go there out of dedication to his mission, that is, to proclaim the "good news" at the center of Jewish life.

Jesus linked the likelihood of his death with total surrender to the arrival of God's kingdom. The historical core of the accounts of the Last Supper (Mk 10:45; Lk 22:47) consists of Jesus' pledge to self-sacrificing service. The *diakonia* Jesus lived is symbolized in his washing of his followers' feet (Lk 12:37b; Jn 13:1-20). Moreover, the Last Supper is a farewell meal. Jesus tells those gathered that this is the last cup he will drink with them until the kingdom comes (Mk 14:25; Lk 22:15-18). With these words, Jesus ties companionship with him in the present to solidarity with him in the future. He urges his disciples to sustain his mission in his absence. Jesus did not seek death, but he did not flee it, for he sensed that his dying was connected with his proclamation of God's gift of compassion.

The Sanhedrin turned Jesus over to the Romans to be condemned to death. Their immediate reason for doing this was that Jesus remained silent when they interrogated him (Mk 14:60-61), and this "critical posture" challenged their authority. Some members of the Sanhedrin may also have judged that Jesus should be sentenced on the basis of Deuteronomy: "The man who acts presumptuously, by not obeying the priest who stands to minister there before the Lord your God, or the judge, that man shall die; so shall you purge evil from Israel" (Dt 17:12). In any case, the Sanhedrin agreed on one thing, that Jesus had to be eliminated. Thus, Jesus of Nazareth was taken to the Roman prefect, Pilate, who sentenced Jesus to death on the charge of sedition.

Jesus was crucified and died a failure. His disciples fled Jerusalem in fear.

The Disciples' Discovery

While the followers of Jesus initially dispersed, they later reassembled at the initiative of Peter. In the aftermath of Jesus' death and burial the disciples underwent a "conversion vision."[13] That is, prior to the traditions of Jesus' appearances and the empty tomb, the disciples gathered together and felt forgiven by Jesus for abandoning him. This reconciliation was a "disclosure situation" in which the disciples "saw" the risen Jesus. Thus began the Easter communities' new understanding of Jesus. In Schillebeeckx's words: "[T]he ground of Christian belief is indubitably Jesus of Nazareth in his earthly proffer of salvation, renewed after his death, now experienced and enunciated by Peter and the Twelve."[14]

I.2 *Narrative, History and Story*

The second section of *Jesus* has received widespread acclaim, from biblical exegetes as well as from theologians. The former have observed the thoroughness and originality of this account of Jesus' ministry and death.[15] They have also questioned, however, Schillebeeckx's neglect of the historical data in John's Gospel and his extensive reliance on a reconstruction of the Q-source and pre-Markan material, since some of this is hypothetical. Theologians acknowledge that this account aids our understanding both of the historical Jesus and of the ways this figure can shape our knowledge of the risen Christ.[16] Similar to the liberal quest, Schillebeeckx has included a review of Jesus' activities in Christology, and yet, in contrast to the original quest, he has done this within the framework of the new quest's recognition that a biography of Jesus cannot be written. But if Schillebeeckx has not given a biography of Jesus, what kind of account has he fashioned?

Schillebeeckx describes his account, "The Gospel of Jesus Christ," as a "post-critical, narrative history."[17] Influenced in part by the critical theory of the Frankfurt School, he is intent on presenting Jesus' ministry and last days without subsuming it into a theory.[18] In "The Gospel of Jesus Christ" he has deliberately avoided any talk about personal existence in general, for this would cast Jesus' life (as it does any life) as an instance of universal principles, and such a view overlooks a life's singular joys and sorrow. Schillebeeckx insists therefore that the way to know about Jesus is through a narrative.

"The Gospel of Jesus Christ" is a narrative, albeit a loose one. It is a recital of events concerning Jesus. It recounts the Baptizer's imprisonment, Jesus' emergence as a public figure, his increasing conflict with the authorities, his last days in Jerusalem, Jesus' death, the flight of the disciples, and their reassembling. This chronology is not tight. Dates and specific details are lacking. But running through these incidents is the thread of Jesus persisting in his preaching of his message and finding this message and himself rejected by many people and authorities, first in Galilee and then in Jerusalem. Loose though this is, it evinces a progression of events in one person's life, and, as a result, it conveys the coherence of this life. It recollects one person's acting, suffering and dying, as well as the initial impact of his life on his followers. It does this with enough detail so that it produces "a relatively coherent picture" of the historical Jesus.

What kind of narrative is this? Schillebeeckx calls it a "history," and I agree with him.[19] In Chapter One, I introduced William Poteat's categories of myth, story and history. What Schillebeeckx has crafted is not a myth, because it is a drama with a beginning and an end in which the characters are not personal archetypes but distinct individuals. Further, "The Gospel of Jesus Christ" is not a story, because it aims at historical accuracy, based upon critical analysis of the Scriptures. While historians and exegetes may want to argue about whether some of the things occurred as Schillebeeckx presents them, they would agree that his individual details and overall account are plausible and arrived at according to the canons of historical study. "The Gospel of Jesus Christ" is therefore a history, for it is, in Poteat's words, a "deployment of events, bound to what we question-beggingly, but unproblematically, and . . . benignly call 'facts'."[20]

The first question of this chapter is now answered. What kind of account of Jesus has Schillebeeckx given in section two of *Jesus?* He calls it a "post-critical, narrative history." Using Poteat's definitions, I describe "The Gospel of Jesus Christ" as an historical narrative, a roughly sketched history. With this classification, we will be able to compare it with the different kinds of narratives that I will employ in later chapters. Let us press on to our second question: How does this historical narrative function in *Jesus?*

II. *The Logic of Disclosure*

On a number of occasions in "The Gospel of Jesus Christ" Schillebeeckx speaks about "disclosure situations."[21] He observes, for example, that Jesus' baptism was probably a moment of disclosure for him. Also, he claims that the resurrection appearances were probably situations of insight in which the disciples "encountered" the risen Christ and experienced a "conversion."[22] Schillebeeckx's use of the notion of disclosure is one major line of argumentation in *Jesus.* According to Schillebeeckx, early Christians identified Jesus as the Son of God on the basis of an insight in which they realized "something more" about this Nazarean. I shall review the logic of disclosure situations, as explicated by Ian T. Ramsey and Alan Richardson, so that we can appreciate how "The Gospel of Jesus Christ" is meant to function as a disclosure situation.[23]

According to Ian T. Ramsey, intellectual discovery is the recognition of a pattern or unity in what appears as a collection of unrelated, discrete elements. It involves perceiving unifying lines where they are not obvious. Ramsey writes: "The situation is more than 'what's seen', it has taken on 'depth'. . . . "[24] He explains further:

> I use 'disclosure' not in relation to information, but to refer to situations about which various metaphorical phrases are commonly used. Such phrases, for example, are those which speak of situations 'coming alive,' 'taking on depth,' situations in which 'the penny drops,' where we 'see' but not with eyes of flesh, where 'something strikes us,' where 'eye meets eye,' where 'heart misses a beat.'[25]

A "situation of disclosure" is one in which we see something more than meets the eye at first glance. It is an occasion when we discern a pattern in a seemingly random collection of data.[26] Insight involves the discovery of a unity where none was obvious. Imagine, for example, a sheet of paper with many dots that at first appear unrelated. But after we look away and then back, we suddenly see an outline. We discern the shape of a turtle. Or, to take another example, we are given a series of numbers, for example, 2, 4, 16, 256, etc. After a moment's thought, we grasp the formula, namely squaring. These two instances remind us that understanding includes the discovery of a coherence in a mass of separate elements. Also, since the knower often has the sense that the insight is not earned but received, another word for "insight" or "discovery" is "disclosure."

According to Ramsey, disclosures occur not only in ordinary matters, but also with regard to the meaning of life itself. This kind of discovery is a "cosmic disclosure." It involves an insight into the "source" that unites the discrete, observable elements of life, whereas other kinds of insight concern particular entities and relationships.

Cosmic or religious knowledge is comprehensive. It discerns the mysterious unity at the heart of all creation. Ramsey writes:

> A cosmic disclosure is a situation which has come alive both subjectively and objectively, where a "plain", "flat" situation restricted to the data of sense experience has taken on "depth" or, as we say, "a new dimension". As a situation takes on depth objectively so I, as subject, take on depth subjectively; I too come alive. . . . There is no supernatural separated by a gulf from the natural, but a supernatural of fulfillment, not denial. Further, the objectivity of God is in the last resort safeguarded as being grounded in that which is *other than myself* in such a cosmic disclosure, where I am aware of an activity meeting my own. In so far as I am aware of being relatively passive, of being acted upon, to that degree I am aware of what confronts me which is other than myself, and it is this which in a fully developed conceptual scheme can be called "god." Such a conceptual scheme arises from interweaving with an eye to comprehension, consistency, coherence and simplicity, the various strands of discourse to which various models, central to cosmic disclosure give rise.[27]

A cosmic disclosure is an insight in which we see a depth and unity in the wealth of phenomena that surround us. Moreover, there is the awareness that we have not imposed this coherence on to the data; rather we have found it there, though not solely through our efforts. What we have come upon has in fact come to us. Also, it is "objective," though not in the way that empirical data and facts are objective, for this reality is not obvious. It is known by insight; it is discovered. What has taken place, says Ramsey, is cosmic or religious disclosure.

To this point, we have seen that disclosure entails seeing something more, an inner unity. Also, this kind of discovery occurs both in mundane matters, for example, in numerical configurations and a pattern in a person's behavior, and also in cosmic matters, for example, in belief in God. Moreover, we have implicitly seen that this process entails at least two steps: first, data is assembled, and, second, an insight is attained into this material. Now, we can consider a third step: expressing the insight.

Once we make a discovery, we need to find the best way to communicate it. Sometimes this is not difficult. For example, when we see the pattern in a numerical series, we simply need to name it, for instance, "squaring numbers." Our expression of an insight gets more difficult, however, when the reality about which we have gained new knowledge is complex. For example, to understand the human mind, we often compare it to a computer. This sophisticated technology provides a way of talking about an even more intricate reality, the mind. In the case of complex realities, we rely on comparisons, on metaphor and analogy to convey our insight. We adopt what Ramsey calls an analog model, that is, a set of images and concepts "with which we are all familiar, and which can be used for reaching another situation with which we are not so familiar; one which, without the model, we should not recognize so easily."[28]

To tie down this discussion, consider this instance of cosmic disclosure, as described by Herman Wouk in his novel *Winds of War*. Captain Victor "Pug" Henry has recently returned to sea. He is delighted about this and finds himself at night standing on his ship's bridge:

On clear nights, no matter how cold the wind and how rough the sea, he spent hours after dinner alone on the flying bridge. The broad dark ocean, the streaming pure air, the crowded stars arching overhead, always made him feel what the Bible called the spirit of God hovering on the face of the waters. Down the years even more than his childhood Bible training, this religious awe inspired by nights at sea had kept Captain Henry a believer. He spoke of this to nobody, not to ministers who were his old friends; he would have felt embarrassed and mawkish, for he was not sure how seriously even they took the Lord. On this voyage, the Almighty was there for Victor Henry as always in the black starry universe, a presence actual and lovable, if disturbingly unpredictable.[29]

This scene exhibits the threefold process of insight, localized in a cosmic disclosure. First, there is a mass of discrete, empirical elements: the dark night, the array of stars, the cold wind, the ocean, the roll of the ship, and the threat of war with Germany. These elements exhibit no blatant ties to one another. Someone else could stand on the ship's bridge beside Captain Henry, see each of the separate elements that Pug sees, and yet not encounter what Pug does. Second, Pug Henry sees a unity binding everything together, including him, and giving meaning to all of the otherwise opaque features. This unifying dynamism is objective, and it has come to him. It is "what the Bible called the spirit of God hovering on the face of the waters." In the process of insight this is step two: Pug sees something more. He discerns the source of unity. Third, this discernment yields an analog model of God: God is "the Almighty." God is the "person" of total power in contrast to the limited power of the captain of a ship. This power shows itself as "a presence actual and lovable, if disturbingly unpredictable."

This example of a cosmic disclosure positions us to consider the character of biblical testimony. The threefold process of insight, as illuminated by Ramsey, can be fruitfully applied to the formation of the Bible. According to Richardson, the foundational experiences of Jewish-Christian belief occurred in what appeared to be ordinary occurrences. The story of the burning bush, the narratives of the exodus, and the recollections of the exile and return sprang from occasions in which the Israelites discerned God in the events of their communal life. Richardson writes:

> Perhaps nothing externally happened in Egypt or at the Red Sea or in the Wilderness which we today would not account for by natural means; perhaps there was no 'miracle' in the Humean sense. But for Israel, and rightly, what happened was miraculous, a disclosure of the divine purpose and an act of divine redemption in the midst of real, 'secular' history, so that Israel could say, as of all the deliverances in her history, 'This is Yahweh's doing, and it is marvelous in our eyes' (Ps. 118:23).[30]

In Richardson's view, the three steps that constitute the ordinary process of disclosure were taken by the believing community, and these eventually led to at least some of the testimony we find in the Bible. First, the people found themselves in what appeared to be an ordinary situation. Second, as they observed the details of the situation, they came to the awareness of God, not unlike Pug Henry in *Winds of War*. And third, these people expressed their discovery of God in analog models.

They took ordinary images (e.g., fire and a bush, water and wind), and they applied them to what was unfamiliar, indeed mysterious.

III. *An Historical and Genetic Method*

The role of the historical narrative in *Jesus* can be illumined by our discussion of disclosure situations and the threefold process of insight. Schillebeeckx is convinced that the first Christians arrived at their confession of Jesus as the Christ by having walked a path of discovery similar to the one we follow for many forms of knowledge. That is, Jesus' disciples first remembered all of Jesus' words and deeds, then they saw something more in this data, and finally they communicated this "something more" through the use of familiar images, for example, being a son or daughter to a loving parent. This path can be walked again today, insists Schillebeeckx, and *Jesus* is meant to help its readers along the journey of this discovery, the *"itinerarium mentis."*[31]

The method in *Jesus* is therefore both "historical," assembling the historical data, and "genetic," imitating the genesis of Christian faith by fostering insight into this data.[32] In other words, Schillebeeckx has designed his "experiment in Christology" according to the threefold process of discovery clarified by Ramsey and Richardson. "The Gospel of Jesus Christ" is meant to reproduce the situation of disclosure that led the early Christian assembly to identify Jesus as the Son of God. We can see this by first looking at the design of *Jesus* and then by reviewing the book's presentation of early models of Jesus.

Jesus consists of four parts.[33] The first is a commentary on the book's aims and methods. It is entitled "Questions of Method, Hermeneutics and Criteria." The second part, as we have already seen, is an historical narrative, "The Gospel of Jesus Christ." The third part, "Christian Interpretation of the Crucified and Risen One," reviews the earliest Christian images of Jesus, for instance, as the prophet of the world's end, the "eschatological prophet." The fourth part treats the conclusions of the book's historical narrative and of its review of early models, thereby giving some clues for new representations of Christ today. It is entitled "Who Do We Say That He Is?"

This structure aligns with the threefold process of discovery outlined by Ramsey.[34] After introducing his aims and approach (Part One),

Schillebeeckx sets the situation of a possible disclosure. This entails recounting the historical narrative about Jesus, "The Gospel of Jesus Christ" (Part Two). This is the first step to a discovery about Jesus. That is, this narrative is analogous to the remembrance of Jesus held by his disciples nearly two thousand years ago. The standard process of insight involves two other steps, both of which are expressed in "Christian Interpretation of the Crucified and Risen One" (Part Three). Here are combined the second and third steps of the insight attained by the first Christians. In hindsight, they discerned a "depth" or unity in the life of the Nazarean, and they articulated this in the images at hand from their Palestinian heritage. This therefore was, says Schillebeeckx, the genesis of Christian faith. That we too can follow this process of discovery today is the claim argued in "Who Do We Say That He Is?" (Part Four).

This view of *Jesus* is confirmed by a statement concluding the book's third part. Here Schillebeeckx gives his rationale for the structure of the book as a whole:

> I do not even think that the theologian needs to find new models [of Jesus]. . . . His job—a serious and responsible one at that—is to gather together elements which may lead to a new, authentic 'disclosure' experience or source experience. For without this disclosure or discovery experience, finding a new model, it seems to me, must be a rather dissociated and pointless Christological chore—whereas a real source experience (one that sees an unfathomable depth disclosed in historically observable data) in being experienced evokes for itself models of its own. In this theology can assist . . . partly by showing how from long ago up to today Christians have attained to such a source experience with regard to Jesus of Nazareth; just as the theologian too—but then formally as a believer (among believers)—may himself come to a 'disclosure' and perhaps be able to make it meaningful and accessible to others. In the concluding Part Four I can only offer a prolegomenon to such an enterprise.[35]

This statement reviews the process of discovery. In saying that the theologian's job is "to gather together elements which may lead to a new, authentic 'disclosure' experience or source experience," Schillebeeckx is speaking about "The Gospel of Jesus Christ" (Part Two). He tells his historical narrative about Jesus in order to reconstruct the situation of recognizing Jesus' full identity. This happened immediately after Jesus' death, and it can occur again today. According to Schillebeeckx, modern women and men can encounter the "living person," Jesus Christ. Indeed, they may have such an experience as they read an historical narrative about Jesus. In any case, such a narrative will introduce them to the starting point and source for Christian belief.

The above statement clarifies further how Part Three relates to Part Two. Having provided the first step, an historical narrative, Schillebeeckx fosters the second and third steps, insight and fresh models, by reviewing early Christians' views and images of Jesus. Schillebeeckx states: "In this theology can assist . . . partly by showing how from long ago up to today Christians have attained to such a source experience with regard to Jesus of Nazareth." Hence, Part Three, entitled "Christian Interpretation of the Crucified-and-Risen One," presents the "four credal models" of the decades after Easter, noting also how these developed out of pre-Christian representations of the latter-day prophet, the Davidic messiah, and the son of man.[36]

Finally, the lengthy statement quoted above also explains the relationship between Schillebeeckx's historical narrative, Part Two, and Part Four, "Who Do We Say That He Is?" In Part Four Schillebeeckx offers some provisional views of Jesus Christ. He anticipates the kind of images and concepts that may emerge among modern Christians once they receive new insight into the figure of the historical Jesus. For example, the Flemish theologian adopts the familiar ideas of compassion, parable and gift when he speaks of Jesus as "the compassion of God," "the parable of God," and "God's gift to all people."[37] In proposing these formulations, he also reiterates the long-standing "model": Jesus is "the Son of God." But in proposing these modern characterizations, Schillebeeckx notes that they are tentative. They are intended to promote his readers' discovery of and witness to Jesus. In the above quotation, he expresses this aim when he states: "In the concluding Part Four I can only offer a prolegomenon to such an enterprise [to working with new models of Jesus]."

In sum, the lengthy quotation above is significant, because it makes clear that Schillebeeckx's historical narrative is the wellspring for the entire book.[38] Part Two is the first step in the threefold process of discovery. Part Three explains how the ancient Church took the second and third steps on the path of understanding Jesus. Part Four anticipates how contemporary Christians may take the second and third steps, discovering anew the full identity of Jesus Christ and conveying this in images that are intelligible in the late twentieth century.

IV. *An Historical Narrative in a Reciprocal Method*

While *Jesus* and *Jesus the Christ* differ in their aims and methods, they are comparable in that both include historical reconstructions of Jesus' ministry, suffering, and death. Schillebeeckx's "The Gospel of Jesus Christ" and Kasper's "The History and Destiny of Jesus Christ" are accounts of the historical Jesus that meet the criteria of modern history. Their formal difference is that Schillebeeckx has molded "The Gospel of Jesus Christ" into an historical narrative, while Kasper uses historical data within an argument of convergence that points to Jesus of Nazareth. Having analyzed the nature and function of Schillebeeckx's account, we can now turn to our third and last question: What would an explicit historical narrative contribute to a reciprocal method, as found in *Jesus the Christ?* We can answer this by first discussing the relation of narrative to image, second by noting the strength of Schillebeeckx's image of Jesus, and third by considering an historical narrative's role in a Christology of reciprocity.

According to Ramsey, insight entails seeing a pattern. The shift from seeing a mass of random items to seeing a unity depends upon the discernment of how these elements are connected. Standing on the ship's bridge, Pug Henry takes in the night sky, stars, briny wind and vast ocean, he senses that these are somehow associated with one another, then he acknowledges their unity: God, "the Almighty." Discovery depends upon an inkling or intuition that there is indeed something to find.[39] It springs from the sense that the discrete items cohere within a whole. Ramsey's emphasis on seeing the threads among the separate elements helps us provisionally appreciate narrative's contribution to our understanding of another person.

Personal identity, as we saw in Chapter One, is the continuity of a life. It is not a fixed point but the development of an initiating, communal, reflective "I." This is a complex reality that we can know in various images or models that show the unity of this life and personality. A narrative aids in our glimpsing this continuity because, as a recital of events, it conveys a sense of the coherence of a life.[40] The connectedness of the narrative highlights links among a life's elements. Thus narrative, especially biography, enables us to move from seeing a person's discrete activities to seeing how these are associated, and this synthesis can in turn produce identifying images of this person.

This reflection on narrative's role in discerning personal identity in general finds a case in point in *Jesus*. Schillebeeckx maintains that historical study can provide theology with an account of Jesus that is independent of the Scripture, tradition and the Church, and this can serve as both an independent point of reference and the source of Christological statements. Schillebeeckx states: "Thus Jesus of Nazareth turns out to be, speaking theologically, the constant anti-pole of the Christ-confessing churches, even though this Opposite Presence—criterion and norm—can never be grasped *per se* but only apprehended in the process whereby the Christian churches let themselves be defined by Jesus."[41]

This is a complex statement, since it suggests, on the one hand, that Jesus can be known apart from the Christian community, and, on the other, that he can only be truly known through the Christian community. For our purposes, we need pursue only one aspect of Schillebeeckx's remarks. That is, in *Jesus*, this "Opposite Presence" is the figure of Jesus as the eschatological prophet, and this view of Jesus is produced by Schillebeeckx's historical narrative. Schillebeeckx's independent criterion, Jesus as the latter-day prophet, emerges from his recital of the events in Jesus' ministry, suffering and death.

The image of the prophet of the last days springs, says Schillebeeckx, from the Deuteronomic assurance that God will bring forth a leader like Moses who will restore Israel: "I will raise up for them a prophet like [Moses] from among their brethren; and I will put my words in his mouth, and he shall speak to them all that I commanded him" (Dt 18:18). The tradition reinforced and refined this model with other elements.[42] This Moses-figure will lead the people out of the land of slavery to the promised land, the new kingdom (Ex 23:20–22). He will have water spring from the rock to nourish the poor and the afflicted (Is 41:18). He will mediate between God and Israel (Dt 5:5), and he would suffer for the people (Dt 9:15–19; Is 42:1f). In all of this, he will be the one anointed by the Spirit and thus called "the anointed," "the Christ."

This representation of Jesus as the latter-day prophet, says Schillebeeckx, runs through the Gospels. During Jesus' life and afterward many of his followers identified Jesus as the eschatological prophet like Moses. For instance, Jesus is presented as "one of the prophets" (Mk 6:15). Some view him as a *propheta redivivus*, for example, as Elijah or John the Baptizer (Mk 8:28). Jesus binds his mission with that of the prophets (Mt 23:29–30), and he compares his destiny with that of a prophet (Lk 11:49–52). Moreover, John's Gospel is designed according to "the prophetic Moses-model."

The image of Jesus as the eschatological prophet looms large in *Jesus*. This portrayal occurs in Part Three, "Christian Interpretation of the Crucified and Risen One." What makes it credible however is the historical narrative that precedes it. "The Gospel of Jesus Christ," that we summarized earlier, provides the pieces of the puzzle and loosely associates them. Jesus heard the preaching of John the Baptizer and was immersed in the Jordan by him. Like a prophet, Jesus proclaimed God's will, as distinct from the mind of many leaders. Also, Jesus acted in ways that displayed the character of the future Israel. He healed the crippled, and he gathered Pharisees, tax collectors and prostitutes at the same table. Jesus performed symbolic gestures, for instance, "cleansing" the temple courtyard. Further, he was misunderstood, rejected and put to death, thereby suffering the fate of some other prophets, for example, Jeremiah. These elements are configured in Schillebeeckx's historical narrative so that they convey the model of the prophet of the world's end.

Schillebeeckx's historical narrative has produced his model of Jesus as the latter-day prophet, but it could also generate others. Part Two, "The Gospel of Jesus Christ," affords more than one image of Jesus. It supports such models of Jesus as the "Davidic Messiah," the "Son of God," and the "son of man." In other words, this historical narrative implies different ways of linking the data about Jesus, and hence it permits the transition from a random collection of material to different insights about Jesus' identity—insights expressed in various models. The narrative does not determine the specific model, but makes initial, tentative links among the data. Further insight leads to the primacy of one representation of Jesus.

Schillebeeckx's work concretely demonstrates the general point that we reached on the basis of Ramsey's thought. Narrative, especially biography, displays the coherence of a life, and therefore it conveys a sense of the ways that a life's incidents are related to the whole of that life. Thus narrative promotes the process of insight, that is, the process of arriving at an identifying image or model of the person. This conclusion has important implications for Christology, as we will see in Chapter Six. For now, this discussion positions us to see how an explicit historical narrative could contribute to Kasper's *Jesus the Christ*.

Kasper agrees with Schillebeeckx in acknowledging that an historical reconstruction can provide Christology with a valid point of reference independent of tradition and the Church. Kasper states: "The church belief instead has in the earthly Jesus, as he is made accessible to us through historical research, a relatively autonomous criterion, a once-and-for all yardstick by which it must continually measure itself."[43] In Kasper's Christology, in contrast to Schillebeeckx's "experiment," historical reconstruction is however only one of Christology's sources. As we have seen, it stands with others, namely with tradition and Scripture as well as with the experience of today's Church. Further, for Kasper history is not Christology's starting point, as it is for Schillebeeckx. Nevertheless, according to Kasper historical research is one essential source for a complete Christology. If it is to play its role as "a relatively autonomous criterion," the study of history must provide an individuating account of Jesus.

The historical image of Jesus in *Jesus the Christ* is not as strong as it could be. The argument of convergence in "The History and Destiny of Jesus Christ" is persuasive, but in pointing to the "figure of unparalleled originality" its outline of this figure remains vague.[44] Kasper's historical review is summed up in the statement "Jesus is the kingdom." But what does this specifically mean? This identifying image is not personal, and without a personal image the historical reference in a reciprocal method remains elusive. In light of Schillebeeckx's historical narrative and our general reflection on narrative and personal identity, we can see that Kasper's approach can be enhanced by making more explicit the narrative embedded in his argument of convergence. Such a narrative, a loose biographical sketch, would produce a stronger historical image of Jesus than is presently conveyed in *Jesus the Christ*.

How would such a narrative function? It would stand as a distinct, though complementary account to those produced from Scripture and tradition and the Church's experience. In Schillebeeckx's genetic method historical study leads to an insight that may produce fresh models of Jesus, from which new Christologies can be developed. An historical narrative's role is quite different in a reciprocal method. In Kasper's kind of endeavor an historical narrative would provide an identifying account of Jesus that, while separate from the testimony of the other sources, could converge with them. Hence, an historical narrative's images of Jesus would not only check any distorting tendencies within the believing community, but would also round out the other representations of Jesus. There would occur a confluence of images of Jesus Christ, as I shall demonstrate in Chapter Five.

According to Kasper, Christology reciprocates between the historical Jesus and the risen Christ by drawing on three sources: history, Scripture and tradition, and today's Church. One of these sources can, we now see, be tapped for data about Jesus that can be shaped into an historical narrative. Our analysis of Schillebeeckx's *Jesus* has shown that a rough biographical sketch of Jesus is possible and that it can produce an identifying image of the Nazarean. This image or model can then represent one of the foci, the historical Jesus, in a Christology of reciprocity. Recognition of an historical narrative's possible contribution to Christology leads to the question whether Christology's other sources also include narratives that could strengthen our attempts to identify Jesus Christ. Frans Jozef van Beeck has shown that systematic inquiry can also turn to tradition for narratives, more specifically for stories about Jesus Christ.

NOTES

1. On the theological significance of the historical Jesus, see: Karl Lehmann, "Die Frage nach Jesus von Nazaret," in: Walter Kern *et al.* (eds.), *Handbuch der Fundamentaltheologie* (Freiburg: Herder, 1985), Vol. II, pp. 122–144; Michael L. Cook, *The Jesus of Faith* (New York: Paulist Press, 1981); Leander Keck, *A Future for the Historical Jesus,* revised edition (Nashville: Abingdon Press, 1981).

2. On Schillebeeckx's life and thought, see: John Bowden, *Edward Schillebeeckx* (New York: Crossroad, 1983); Benedict Viviano, "What Does Schillebeeckx's *Jesus/Christ* Have To Say to a Christian on the Way?," an unpublished paper, given at The Aquinas Institute, St. Louis (1981); T. Mark Schoof, "Dutch Catholic Theology," *Cross Currents,* XXII (1973), 415–427; *idem,* "Masters in Israel: VII. The Later Theology of Edward Schillebeeckx,"

Clergy Review, LV (1970), 943–960; Boniface Willems, "Edward Schillebeeckx," in: Hans Jurgen Schultz (ed.), *Tendenzen der Theologie im 20. Jahrhundert* (Stuttgart: Kreuz, 1966), pp. 602–607.

3. Edward Schillebeeckx, *Jesus*, trans. by H. Hoskins (New York: Seabury, 1979). For the author's informal comments on *Jesus*, see: Edward Schillebeeckx (with Huub Oosterhuis and Piet Hoogeveen), *God Is New Each Moment*, trans. D. Smith (New York: The Seabury Press, 1983), pp. 19–33. A concise statement of this Christology is found in: Edward Schillebeeckx, *Interim Report on the Books "Jesus" and "Christ,"* trans. by J. Bowden (New York: Crossroad, 1981), pp. 105–142.

4. Soteriology is one of Schillebeeckx's primary concerns in *Jesus*, for, as he mentions, he originally intended to entitle the book "Salvation in Jesus Coming from God" (p. 557; cf. pp. 24, 35, 104, 616–625, 669). Cf. Tadahiko Iwashima, *Menschheitsgeschichte und Heilserfahrung* (Düsseldorf: Patmos, 1982).

5. Walter Kasper, "Liberale Christologie," *Evangelischer Kommentar*, VI (1976), 357–360. Kasper's view is similar to that of: Reginald Fuller, "The Historical Jesus," *The Thomist*, XLVIII (July, 1984), 368–382; George W. Stroup, *Jesus Christ for Today* (Philadelphia: Westminster Press, 1982), pp. 73–75.

6. Schillebeeckx, *Interim Report* pp. 64–104, 95.

7. *Ibid.*, p. 97.

8. Alister E. McGrath, *The Making of Modern German Christology* (New York: Basil Blackwell, 1986), pp. 9–93; Norman Perrin, *Rediscovering the Teaching of Jesus* (New York: Harper and Row, 1976), pp. 207–248.

9. Schillebeeckx, *Jesus*, pp. 77–80, 77. Cf. John P. Galvin, "Schillebeeckx: Retracing the Story of Jesus," *Worldview*, XXIV (April 1981), 10–12; *idem*, book review of *Jesus*, *The Heythrop Journal*, XXI (1980), 185–190.

10. *Ibid.*, pp. 105–397.

11. Cf. John P. Galvin, "The Uniqueness of Jesus and His 'Abba Experience' in the Theology of Edward Schillebeeckx," in: Luke Salm (ed.), *The Proceedings of the Catholic Theological Society*, XXXV (1981), 309–314.

12. Cf. John P. Galvin, "The Death of Jesus in the Theology of Edward Schillebeeckx," *The Irish Theological Quarterly*, L (1983/84), 168–180; *idem*, "Jesus' Approach to Death," *Theological Studies*, XLI (1980), 713–744.

13. Schillebeeckx, *Jesus*, p. 385. Cf. Gerald O'Collins, *Interpreting Jesus* (New York: Paulist Press, 1984), pp. 120–124; John P. Galvin, "The Resurrection of Jesus in Contemporary Catholic Systematics," *The Heythrop Journal*, XX (1979), 123–145.

14. Schillebeeckx, *Jesus*, pp. 390–391.

15. Cf. George MacRae, book review of *Jesus*, *Religious Studies Review*, V (October 1979), 270–273; Donald Senior, "Jesus, God's Living Parable,"

Commonweal CVI (March 16, 1979), 147–150; A.L. Descamps, "Comptes rendu," *Revue Théologique de Louvain,* VI (1975), 212–223.

16. Cf. Leo Scheffczyk, "Christology in the Context of Experience," *The Thomist,* XLVIII (July 1984), 383–408; Marcus Lefebure, "Schillebeeckx's Anatomy of Experience," *The New Blackfriars,* LXIV (1983) 270–286; John C. Haughey, "Theological Table-Talk: Schillebeeckx's Christology," *Theology Today,* XXXVIII (1981), 201–207; Leander Keck, *A Future for the Historical Jesus,* pp. 267–278; Brian McDermott, "Roman Catholic Christology," *Theological Studies,* XLI (1980), 339–367; Eugene TeSelle, book review, *Religious Studies Review,* V (October 1979), 267–270; Walter Löser, book review of *Jesus, Theologie und Philosophie,* LI (1976), 257–266; Robert Schreiter, "Christology in the Jewish-Christian Encounter," *Journal of the American Academy of Religion,* XLIV (1976), 693–703.

17. Schillebeeckx, *Jesus,* p. 77.

18. Cf. Robert J. Siebert, *The Critical Theory of Religion* (New York: Walter de Gruyter, 1983); Francis Schüssler Fiorenza, "Critical Social Theory and Christology," *Proceedings of the Catholic Theological Society of America,* XXX (1975), 63–110; Martin Jay, *The Dialectical Imagination* (Boston: Little, Brown and Company, 1973).

19. Schillebeeckx, *Interim Report,* p. 32.

20. William Poteat, "Myths, Stories, History, Eschatology and Action," in: Thomas Langford and W. Poteat (eds.), *Intellect and Hope* (Durham: Duke University Press, 1968), pp. 198–231, 220.

21. Schillebeeckx, *Jesus,* pp. 75, 115, 137, 223, 387, 481, 571, 634, 640, 742.

22. *Ibid.,* pp. 276, 321, 346, 352, 378, 380, 390, 530.

23. On Ramsey's discussion of disclosure situations, see: Terrence W. Tilley, *Talking of God* (New York: Paulist, 1978), pp. 79–92; James W. McClendon, Jr., and James M. Smith, *Understanding Religious Convictions* (Notre Dame: University of Notre Dame Press, 1975), pp. 35–48; Robert H. King, *The Meaning of God* (Philadelphia: Westminster, 1973), pp. 1–21; Thomas Fawcett, *The Symbolic Language of Religion* (Minneapolis: Augsburg, 1971), pp. 173–181.

24. Ian T. Ramsey, *Religious Language* (London: SCM Press, 1957), pp. 11–48, 20.

25. Ian T. Ramsey, "Facts and Disclosures," in: Jerry H. Gill (ed.), *Christian Empiricism* (Grand Rapids: William B. Eerdmanns, 1974), p. 159.

26. Ramsey, *Religious Language,* p. 20.

27. Ian T. Ramsey, "Theology Today and Spirituality Today," in: Eric James (ed.), *Spirituality Today* (London: SCM, 1968), pp. 82–83; quoted in Tilley, *Talking of God,* pp. 81–82.

28. Ramsey, *Religious Language*, p. 61; cf. *idem, Models and Mystery* (New York: Oxford University Press, 1964), p. 4.

29. Herman Wouk, *Winds of War* (Boston: Little, 1971), p. 666.

30. Alan Richardson, *History, Sacred and Profane* (Philadelphia: Westminster, 1964), pp. 224–225. A comparison between Schillebeeckx's work and Richardson's is also made by John Bowden, *Edward Schillebeeckx*, p. 146.

31. On the *itinerarium mentis*, see: Schillebeeckx, *Interim Report*, p. 31. Cf. Louis Dupre, "Experience and Interpretation," *Theological Studies*, XXXXIII (1982), 30–51.

32. Schillebeeckx, *Interim Report*, pp. 34, 97.

33. For an analysis of the structure of *Jesus*, see: John Nijenhuis, "Christology Without Jesus of Nazareth Is Ideology," in: Leonard Swidler (ed.), *Consensus in Theology?* (Philadelphia: Westminster Press, 1980), pp. 125–140.

34. Schillebeeckx appeals to the work of T.S. Kuhn, I. Lakatos, Feyerabend, K. Popper, and the Erlangen School; cf. Schillebeeckx, *Interim Report*, pp. 17–19; cf. *idem*, "Can Christology Be an Experiment?" in: Luke Salm (ed.), *The Proceedings of the Catholic Theological Society*, XXXV (1981), pp. 1–14.

35. Schillebeeckx, *Jesus*, p. 571.

36. *Ibid.*, p. 403.

37. *Ibid.*, p. 650.

38. A critique of Schillebeeckx's way of applying the notion of disclosure to Christian faith is given by Van Harvey, *The Historian and the Believer* (New York: Macmillan, 1966), 246–291.

39. Cf. Bernard Lonergan, *Insight* (New York: Philosophical Library, 1970), pp. 3–13, 283–287.

40. Cf. Arthur C. Danto, *Analytical Philosophy of History* (Cambridge: Cambridge University Press, 1965), pp. 233–253; Schillebeeckx, *Interim Report*, p. 32.

41. Schillebeeckx, *Jesus*, p. 76.

42. *Ibid.*, pp. 475–499; cf. *idem, Interim Report*, pp. 64–69.

43. Walter Kasper, *Jesus the Christ*, trans. V. Green (New York: Paulist Press, 1976), p. 35.

44. *Ibid.*, p. 65.

Chapter Four

THE SYNOPTIC STORY

The Gospels play a key role in the Church's knowledge of Jesus Christ. The testimonies of Matthew, Mark, Luke and John hold a central place at the Eucharist. They serve as the chief source by which Christians remember their Lord, and, in remembering him, meet him again. The Gospels are regarded by the Christian assembly as more than ancient documents from which historical material can be dug out. To a large extent, they are heard as stories, as aesthetic wholes, whose message is grasped by following the sense of their words. For the faithful, the Gospels are stories that convey who Jesus Christ is, that he calls others to follow him, and that he will return.[1]

This view of the Gospels has significance for Christology. If the Church's understanding of Jesus Christ is determined in part by Matthew's, Mark's, Luke's and John's figurations of the Lord, then a systematic inquiry into the person and work of this Lord should also be shaped by the Gospels as stories. In recent decades, theologians have rightly sought to incorporate historical research into their work, and, as we saw in our study of Edward Schillebeeckx's *Jesus,* their labor has borne impressive fruit. Still, an historical approach to the Bible can be filled out by a literary approach that calls attention to what a text means on its own terms.[2] In adopting interpretation of this sort, theologians treat the Scriptures in a way analogous to one of the ways Christians at worship listen to them.[3] In this fourth chapter, I shall argue that Christology is strengthened when it includes literary interpretation of the Bible, specifically, the retelling of the Gospels as stories.

Frans Jozef van Beeck's *Christ Proclaimed* demonstrates this method of interpretation. In this work, van Beeck locates Christology within the Church's worship and service, for he maintains that we can improve our systematic reflections on Jesus Christ by maintaining their bonds to the living dialogue between the risen Lord and the Christian community. In van Beeck's words: "Personal response to Christ is the setting of all cognitive Christological statements. This personal response is conveyed by the rhetorical elements in Christology."[4] One of the chief "rhetorical elements" or linguistic forms upon which van Beeck relies in his Christology is story.[5] The point of departure for his presentation on Jesus Christ as "the man for others" is the "Synoptic story," that is, the narrative held in common by Matthew, Mark and Luke. By examining *Christ Proclaimed,* we shall discern what the Gospels as stories contribute not only to van Beeck's text, but also to a work like Walter Kasper's *Jesus the Christ.*

The theological methods of van Beeck and Kasper are comparable, for both are anchored in the kerygma. Christian proclamation is, insists van Beeck, Christology's primary wellspring, and it is complemented by historical research and contemporary culture.[6] As we saw in Chapter Two, Kasper too has pinpointed these same three sources: Scripture and tradition, history and modern thought. Moreover, not only have both theologians commented on the importance of these three sources, they also agree in their actual use of two of them. Early Christian testimony and the experience of today's Church are the dominant sources throughout *Christ Proclaimed* and also in the third major section, "The Mystery of Jesus Christ," of *Jesus the Christ.*

A chief difference between van Beeck's work and Kasper's stems from the degree to which each employs historical research. Whereas an historical reconstruction of Jesus' ministry, life and death constitutes the second major section in *Jesus the Christ,* it is not found in *Christ Proclaimed.* These two Christologies can therefore be described in this way: *Christ Proclaimed* is a kerygmatic Christology, for it focuses primarily on the risen Lord, and *Jesus the Christ* is a Christology of reciprocity, for it treats both the historical Jesus and the post-Easter Christ.[7]

The pros and cons of these distinct Christologies do not concern us here. Rather, I want to analyze the character and purpose of one major component in *Christ Proclaimed,* and then propose how this might also contribute to a work like *Jesus the Christ. Christ Proclaimed* includes a retelling of the Synoptic story.[8] This recollection of the narrative running through the Gospels of Matthew, Mark and Luke serves as the starting point for a systematic inquiry into Jesus' person and work. In contrast, while *Jesus the Christ* refers to scriptural stories, for example, to Philippians 2:6–11 and Romans 5:12–21, it does not explicitly recollect them. Therefore, I propose that a Christology of reciprocity would better accomplish its aim of identifying Jesus Christ if it imitated the kerygmatic Christology's obvious use of story. To see this, let us pursue three questions, the same ones previously posed in our analysis of Schillebeeckx's work. First, what kind of account of Jesus is operative in *Christ Proclaimed?* Second, how does it function in this work? Third, how would an account of this sort enhance an endeavor like *Jesus the Christ?*

I. *Gospel as Story*

The Gospels are narratives. They recollect a series of events within an account that has a beginning, a middle and an end. More specifically, the Gospels are neither myths nor histories, for their events are neither archetypal nor tied to the facts. The Gospels are stories. They recount a series of events in such a way as to require the concepts "happen," "person" and "action," but without being primarily concerned about conveying all of the historical data demanded of a history.[9] This is not to say however that the Gospels are fiction, in the sense of constructions of an imaginary world. The Gospels tell of a drama set in a specific historical time and place, and their characters actually existed. They unite facts and biblical allusions in order to witness to a truth that surpasses the limits of history. Thus, the Gospels can be aptly classified as nonfiction stories. This view of the Gospels is expressed in *Christ Proclaimed.*

A narrative, observes Frans Jozef van Beeck, stands at the center of Christian faith. This is not however a history, but a story—indeed, a "witnessing story." It is a recollection that attests to the actions of Jesus Christ and the response of those committed to him. This story is told not primarily to establish empirical details about this Jesus, but to communicate a community's conviction and insight about this man. It can be compared, states van Beeck, to a lover's remembrance of the beloved:

> Furthermore, just as a lover spontaneously turns his autobiography into a testimony to his beloved, the Christian self-expression will be a witnessing story about Christ. Because the point is neither the beloved's nor Jesus' biography, the story

will be pre-critical; historical accuracy is not the point. The point is that the narrator of the story identifies himself under invocation, in the name of the person who, by encountering him, has called for the identity he now enjoys and wants to express and share. Hence, the story told will be a *significant story,* not a critical narrative account.[10]

This "significant story" is, van Beeck points out, part of the Church's proclamation. We tend to regard kerygma solely as announcement, but this reduces the message to teaching and exhortation when in fact it also entails recollection. The kerygma includes "homologia," testimony in the form of a "narrative recital" of Jesus' words and deeds. The Dutch theologian states:

What we have been accustomed, since [Charles Harold] Dodd, to call the *kerygma . . .* is in fact not just the apostolic preaching—the Spirited call to conversion and obedience of faith in Christ alive—but first and foremost it is the Christian *homologia,* the narrative recital, in praise of God, through Jesus Christ, on the strength of the Spirit, of the great things God has done among us.[11]

Because kerygma is also homologia, it is a story with three characteristics. First, it attests to a present and future "person." It is not solely about a past figure. Second, kerygma speaks about God as well as Jesus Christ. God has acted in the life of Jesus Christ. Third, it tells not only about Jesus' actions, but also about the responses of the witnesses, among whom stands the one proclaiming the good news.

These elements are manifest even in the short formula passed on by Paul:

[. . .] the gospel of God [. . .] concerning his Son, who was descended from David according to the flesh and designated Son of God in power according to the Spirit of holiness by his resurrection from the dead, Jesus Christ our Lord, through whom we have received grace and apostleship to the law of Moses and from the prophets (Rom 1:1–4).

This account from Paul's Letter to the Romans is a story. It recounts in a formulaic way a sequence of events, agents and their deeds. In doing this, it manifests three features. First, Jesus Christ stands in the present and future due to "his resurrection from the dead." As van Beeck puts it: "[T]he telling of the story is a testimonial invocation warranted by the Resurrection."[12] Second, this drama is not that of Jesus alone. He "was designated Son of God in power according to the Spirit." God was involved here. Again, to quote van Beeck: "[T]he life of Jesus was a climactic journey, marked by goodness to others and struggle with the powers that be, and ending in final rejection followed by vindication." This implies that God vindicates Jesus. Third, the proclaimer-narrator is part of the recollection. What has occurred has engaged those who attest to it. Hence, the formula reads: "[W]e have received grace and apostleship to the law of Moses and from the prophet." The proclaimer's involvement in the message is, contends van Beeck, significant: "[T]he implication for the Church is that the story of Jesus provides her with a programmatic parallel to her own life." These three features display the complexity of what is "a witnessing story about Christ" and "the ultimate glorification of the Father."[13]

Along with the short formula in Romans 1, the story of Jesus Christ has assumed longer forms. One of these is expressed, notes van Beeck, in the Acts of the Apostles:

> You know the word which he sent to Israel, preaching good news of peace by Jesus Christ (he is Lord of all), the word which was proclaimed throughout all Judea, beginning from Galilee after the baptism which John preached: how God anointed Jesus of Nazareth with the Holy Spirit and with power; how he went about doing good and healing all that were oppressed by the devil, for God was with him. And we are witnesses to all that he did both in the country of the Jews and in Jerusalem. They put him to death by hanging him on a tree; but God raised him on the third day and made him manifest; not to all the people but to us who were chosen by God as witnesses, who ate and drank with him after he rose from the dead. And he commanded us to preach to the people, and to testify that he is the one ordained by God to be judge of the

living and the dead (Acts 10:36–42; cf. Acts 13:23–25, 27–31).

This longer form, like the short one, is also a story. It recounts events, persons and their actions. Further, it evinces the "triple agenda" of the short formula.[14] First, it speaks of the one raised from the dead. He is not solely a past figure, for since his resurrection he has "commanded us to preach to the people, and to testify that he is the one ordained by God to be judge of the living and the dead." Second, it praises God who displayed once-and-for all the bountiful love that has been recounted in other stories, for example, those in Genesis about Abraham, Isaac and Jacob and those in Exodus about Moses. This God anointed Jesus "with the Holy Spirit," remained with Jesus throughout his ministry, and "raised him on the third day and made him manifest." Third, this kerygmatic statement recounts how the story's narrators are themselves part of the story. God chose them "as witnesses." In response therefore to God and Jesus Christ, they proclaim this good news, and in proclaiming this message in word and deed, the witnesses themselves have become part of the story.

Even though a story is a recital of events, not bound to the "facts," it can express an objective reality. It can describe a unity or pattern beyond the scope of history. In *Christ Proclaimed,* van Beeck has called our attention to the story that constitutes the kerygma. It is not, as he says, "a critical narrative account" of Jesus, though such an account may also be constructed about Jesus. Rather, this literary unit is a testimony, "a witnessing story," that tells of the actions of Christ, God's intervention in human affairs, and the proclaimer's involvement in this saving drama.

II. *An Identifying Story*

The testimonies found in Romans 1 and Acts 10 are not of course the only versions of the kerygma. Another form is the Gospels. Matthew, Mark, Luke, and John are stories, and, like the shorter forms of the good news, they too attest to the risen Christ's actions, God's agency and the narrator's involvement. Moreover, they provide identifying characterizations of the story's key figures, for example, of Jesus and

Peter. The Gospels, especially the Synoptic Gospels, possess what modern literary critics call "realism," the style of depicting the give-and-take between characters and their settings in such a way that the narrative gains depth, appears lifelike.[15] As a result, the characters emerge in the drama as concrete persons with intentions, complex emotions and histories. The theological significance of the Synoptic Gospels' realism has been discussed by van Beeck who in part draws on the work of Hans Frei and David Kelsey.

According to van Beeck, the Synoptic Gospels' vivid depictions of Jesus identify the one whom Christians address as Lord. Matthew, Mark and Luke describe Jesus' interactions with other persons, events and setting in such detail that Jesus' character is manifest. The Gospels' realism yields lifelike portraits that equip Christians to say who Jesus Christ is. Van Beeck states:

> To know who Jesus is we do not necessarily need descriptive, factual answers to strictly historical questions, nor do we need direct biographical information about the personality, inner motivation, or even the ethical quality of Jesus. To realize who "this Jesus" is, all we need is a story, a realistic narrative, for it is characteristic of realistic narrative to present the identity of a subject by means of a fusion of intention and circumstance.[16]

Van Beeck's point is crucial to Christology. Once we acknowledge the Gospels' realism, we can appreciate these stories as aesthetic wholes that can guide our attempts to identify Jesus Christ. With this recognition, we would focus on the protagonist portrayed in the text. We would not be primarily oriented to the historical personage to whom the Gospels refer, nor would we interpret the texts primarily on the basis of their redactor's intention and setting. In our effort to know Jesus Christ, we would attend to the ways he is described in the Gospels.

This recognition of the Gospels' literary character and its implications for Christology lies at the heart of *Christ Proclaimed*. Background to this is provided by Hans Frei's *The Eclipse of Biblical Narrative* and *The Identity of Jesus Christ* and also by David Kelsey's *The Uses of Scripture in Recent Theology*.[17]

Frei has called attention to the "history-like" quality of many biblical narratives.[18] Accounts like the Synoptic Gospels closely resemble history. They seriously represent the commonplace world by means of the interplay of characters and their circumstances. In support of this view, Frei appeals to the classic study *Mimesis* (1946) in which Erich Auerbach describes realism as follows:

> The serious treatment of everyday reality, the rise of more extensive and socially inferior human groups to the position of subject matter for problematic-existential representation, on the one hand; on the other the embedding of random persons and events in the general course of contemporary history, the fluid historical background—these, we believe, are the foundations of modern realism. . . . [19]

The Gospels' realism shapes the way they present their major characters. In these narratives persons are agents; they enact their intentions, thereby showing their identity as they interact with one another and events within their changing situations. In Kelsey's words: "Moreover, what one knows about the story's central agent is not known by 'inference' from the story. On the contrary, he is known quite directly in and with the story, and recedes from cognitive grasp the more he is abstracted from the story."[20]

Quite concretely, therefore, Jesus is known in the Gospels by what he says, does and endures within a world of political and religious rivalry. He tells parables, he heals cripples, he puts up with the disciples' incomprehension, and he is put to death by the authorities. In this, Jesus' primary aim in life, indeed his very self, is exhibited: he lives to bring in "the kingdom of God." He is the "Son of God." Hence, the Gospels are "identity descriptions" of Jesus.[21]

This realism has bearing upon the way the Gospels ask to be read. They draw us into their world, demanding that we take them on their own terms. According to Auerbach, a biblical narrative is "in need of interpretation on the basis of its own content." Frei puts it this way: "[W]hat [the gospels] tell us is the fruit of the stories themselves. We cannot have what they are about ('the subject matter') without the stories themselves."[22] Further, acknowledging the Bible's realism, George Lindbeck wonders "whether Scripture does not perhaps supply its own interpretive framework."[23] In a word, the weaving of character and setting and events in the evangelists' stories about Jesus means that the Gospels' content and form are inseparable. If we want to know the Gospels' Jesus, we need to read the story in which he is the central agent.

This view of the Gospels sheds light on their roles, first, in the Christian life and, second, in theology. First, as noted earlier, when Christians gather in worship, they tend to hear the Gospels as stories. Matthew, Mark, Luke and John present the assembly with images, indeed identifying descriptions, of the person in whom it is united and with whom it gives praise and thanks to God. These individuating accounts equip the Church to discern and respond to the risen Lord. Summarizing Karl Barth's thought on Scripture in the Christian life, Kelsey writes:

> Sometimes, when used in church as the basis of preaching and worship, the texts may provide the occasion on which the revelatory event occurs here and now and God ''speaks as *I* and addresses as *thou.*'' On such occasions the stories ''work.'' The agent they render is truly made present to the worshipper in a revelatory encounter. [24]

Second, recognition of the Gospels as realistic stories raises the issue of their roles in recent theology. In *The Eclipse of Biblical Narrative,* Frei has convincingly argued that since the rise of the historical critical methods theologians have not known how to interpret biblical stories as stories. [25] Prior to the 1700's we took these accounts on their word. We regarded literal interpretation as the primary form after which we could adopt others, for example, allegorical interpretation. With higher criticism, however, we could no longer take the biblical testimony as a ''factual'' description of what occurred. For example, when we apply historical critical methods to the Gospels, we realize that these accounts are not biographies. We can rely on them as sources for an historical review of the sort given by Schillebeeckx. Since we cannot read them as we would a history, though, we have tended to go behind them, not taking them on their own terms.

This way of treating biblical narratives has remained unsatisfactory to those who have acknowledged their literary nature. As Frei notes, throughout the development of higher criticism scholars have taken note of the history-like character of large segments of the Bible. They observed that, as a result of its realism, the Bible asks that its narratives be read according to the sense of the words. "[W]e are to fit our own life," observes Auerbach, "into [the Bible's] world, feel ourselves to be elements in its structure of universal history."[26] But how do we do this without sacrificing the intellectual integrity of the historical-critical methods? We have been puzzled therefore about how our scriptural interpretation could acknowledge the Bible's realism. Frei writes:

> But commentators, especially those influenced by historical criticism, virtually to a man failed to understand what they had seen when they had recognized the realistic character of biblical narratives, because every time they acknowledged it they thought this was identical with affirming not only the history-likeness but also a degree of historical likelihood of the stories.[27]

Faced with the Bible's history-like accounts, scholars have responded in different ways. Some of them have upheld the view that the Bible must be read literally, in a manner which equates the verbal sense with the historical referent. To do this, they have set strict limits on the use of historical-critical methods. Other scholars have regarded biblical texts as sources from which we can extract historical data and, perhaps, an insight into human existence. They do not read Scripture on its own terms, for this would conflict with the presuppositions of modern historical methods. But in choosing not to read biblical narratives according to their verbal sense, these scholars have neglected a significant feature of these texts, namely their narrative character. As Frei points out, scriptural texts' "specifically realistic characteristic, though acknowledged by all hands to be there, finally came to be ignored, or—even more fascinatingly—its presence or distinctiveness came to be denied for lack of a 'method' to isolate it."[28]

Where then do we go from here? How do we interpret the Gospels in such a way as to acknowledge their realism? We can incorporate the literary analysis of the Bible into our theology. We can make Scripture's identifying descriptions of Jesus part of our systematic investigations.

One form of this literary rendering of biblical narratives appears in Barth's writings. In the *Church Dogmatics,* the great Reformed theologian calls attention to the Gospels as stories and then employs these stories in his theological reflection. As Kelsey's analysis shows, this occurs in the presentation on the humanity of Christ in "The Royal Man," *Church Dogmatics,* IV/2.[29] Barth does not go behind the Gospels to the historical figure of Jesus; he attends solely to the person portrayed in the Gospels. He insists that Jesus' identity is exhibited in his acts, as these are recounted by the evangelists, and their patterns of description converge, Barth observes, in the passion narrative. Here is depicted the one act, Jesus' suffering and death, in which Jesus unambiguously reveals who and what he is. Describing Barth's scriptural interpretation in "The Royal Man," Kelsey states:

> Indeed, it is as though Barth took scripture to be one vast, loosely structured non-fictional novel. . . . The characteristic patterns in the narrative guide what the theologian says about the agent/subject of the stories, in much the way that patterns in a novel guide what a literary critic may say about the characters in the novel.[30]

The Gospels are to be taken as "one, loosely structured non-fictional novel" that provide identifying descriptions of Jesus. While Barth also adopts other forms of interpretation along with this literary approach, this one stands out since it calls attention to what many theologians have overlooked, the Gospels as stories.

Other theologians have adopted Barth's approach to the Bible in their systematic investigations. Frei has relied on a literary interpretation of the Synoptic Gospels in *The Identity of Jesus Christ.* Moreover, van Beeck has employed a similar hermeneutics in *Christ Proclaimed,* and it is to this work that we can now return. At the outset of this chapter we asked: How does van Beeck view the Gospels? And, in light of the work of Barth, Frei and Kelsey, we have reached an answer. In *Christ Proclaimed* van Beeck regards the Gospels as realistic stories that convey who Jesus Christ is. Our second question is: How do the Gospels contribute to van Beeck's theological inquiry?

III.1 *A Kerygmatic Method*

Christ Proclaimed sets Christology within the Church's Christ-centered life. It highlights the continuity between the Christian community's

response to the risen Christ—a response made in liturgy and service—
and Christology in the strict sense. To appreciate van Beeck's use of the
Gospels therefore we need to understand his overall program. Once this
is clear, then we can review how the synoptic story is retold in *Christ
Proclaimed* and analyze how this recollection produces van Beeck's conceptual presentation on Jesus' identity.

Christology, contends van Beeck, is a linguistic activity that occurs
in response to the risen Lord. It is not a speculative endeavor done apart
from the Christian assembly. Christology flows out of the Church's worship and witness, and therefore it must be understood in relation to these
sources. Van Beeck's "main thesis" is therefore "that all christological
discernments are only correctly understood if they are set against the
background of a worshipful, witnessing act of total surrender to Jesus
Christ alive in the Spirit, who accepts, purifies, and places in perspective
all human concerns."[31]

The book's direction is indicated by its subtitle, *Christology as
Rhetoric*. Drawing on the linguistic studies of I. T. Ramsey, J. W. M.
Verhaar, D. Evans and J. Barr, van Beeck presents Christology as a
speech-act entailing various forms of discourse, that is, both figurative
speech and thematic language.[32] Christology is "intersubjective"; it
possesses many of the features of a dialogue. As van Beeck states: "This
book . . . considers Christological statements primarily as expressions
of dialogue among persons in dialectical response both to the living Lord
and to the concerns of their cultures. . . . "[33] Just as an ordinary con-
versation between two people consists of names, metaphors, propositions, and stories, so too, systematic theology can include these modes
of speech.

An analogy for van Beeck's view is, as he notes, one lover's relating to the beloved. The most important talk is that which occurs directly
between the lover and the beloved. The first level of reflection on this
dialogue is the lover's testimony about the beloved. This testimony involves telling the story of their love. This is comparable to the Church's
worship and service, which include recounting the story of Jesus Christ
and living in a way parallel to it. As van Beeck says: "[J]ust as a lover
spontaneously turns his autobiography into a testimony to his beloved,
the Christian self-expression will be a witnessing story about Christ."[34]
The second level of reflection is the lover's thought about love in general—this thought however springs from one specific love and is fruitful

insofar as it gains insight into this specific love. This is comparable to the Church's theological statements. They arise from the encounter with Jesus Christ, and they are worthwhile to the extent that they shed new light on Jesus Christ and his union with humankind. In short, Christology is a speech-act; it expresses the "goal" of a community's way of life, and it directs the community toward this goal.[35]

To argue his thesis, van Beeck structures *Christ Proclaimed* in three major parts. In the first part (the introduction and chapters one and two), he invites readers to undergo a mental "conversion," to broaden their view of theology so that it includes a functional view of language as well as a referential view.[36] Words not only mean by pointing to objects, they also mean by their use, and this needs to be kept in mind if we are to grasp the meaning of theology's conceptual terms, for example, of "person."

In the book's second part (chapters three through seven), van Beeck sets Christology within the Christian life. The Church lives out of its encounter with the risen Christ, and this encounter shapes the Church's "rhetoric," its speaking and doing.[37] As a result, the ascribing of Christological titles to Jesus springs from the awareness that Jesus Christ has embodied all human concerns. This is "the rhetoric of inclusion." Also, talk about the "person" of Jesus Christ comes from the recognition that Jesus surrendered himself to God and that it is our task to do likewise. This is "the rhetoric of obedience." Moreover, the language of the resurrection reflects the knowledge that all human aspirations will be fulfilled through Jesus Christ. This is "the rhetoric of hope." All of the Church's technical language, then, has its roots in the living dialogue between the risen Christ and the Christian assembly.

The book's third part consists of what is customarily called systematic theology, specifically Christology. At the outset (chapter eight), van Beeck positions this investigation in relation to Jesus' resurrection. Then (chapter nine) he begins his "thematic reflection" by recalling the story of Jesus Christ, as told in the Epistle to the Romans and the Acts of the Apostles.[38] Next, van Beeck pursues two questions. First, who is the person presented in the Synoptic story (chapter ten)? Second, what is the source of this person's life (chapter eleven)? The answers to these queries provide the basis for further considerations on Christian ethics (chapter twelve) and worship (chapter thirteen). For our purposes, we need only concentrate on van Beeck's literary rendering of the Synoptic story (chapter ten) and conceptual presentation on Jesus' identity (chapter eleven).

III.2 The Synoptic Story

Who is the person portrayed by Matthew, Mark and Luke? He is distinguished, says van Beeck, through his interaction with his situation. In the give-and-take with his disciples, the people and the authorities, this Jesus emerges as a singular individual. At the start of his ministry, he announces the coming of the kingdom, and he shows its fruit through his miracles. Yet, those who see his deeds and hear his words do not solely attend to Jesus' message, they also wonder about him. From the outset they ask: Who is this? Is he not the carpenter's son? "Thus the issue of Jesus' individuality is raised," observes van Beeck, "in the context of the way in which he addresses himself, with his message, to others."[39]

Moreover, Jesus cares for these people and understands them. In van Beeck's words: "He has an inner, sympathetic awareness of the predicament of the people: he identifies their concerns with unfailing precision; he heals them by the power of the Spirit."[40] As the story unfolds, however, the disciples, the people and the authorities increasingly misunderstand Jesus. Some want him to assume kingly power, others take him as Beelzebul, and others are puzzled. For his part, Jesus persists in linking himself to the kingdom and reaching out to others, and, for this, he is increasingly ostracized by the people.

This isolation is telling. On the one hand, it reveals Jesus' character. He continues to care for people, though they spurn him. On the other hand, Jesus' rejection acts as a mirror that reflects the self-concern of the disciples, people and authorities. "In the very act of failing to recognize Jesus, those around him are revealed as people who would live by self-established assurance rather than by faith."[41] On the one hand, Jesus is a man for others, and, on the other, he is the man misunderstood and hated by others. He becomes individuated as he loves others and accepts their inhumanity toward him.

The interaction between Jesus and his world comes to its climax in Jerusalem. Van Beeck writes: "He does not try to beat his opponents. . . . He predicts his disciples' flight. He predicts his betrayal; he addresses Judas as 'friend'.''[42] Jesus chooses not to flee from the authorities, but to give himself over to them, to stand in their presence. ''His repeated 'You have said so' confronts the high priest and Pilate with their own words. His glance after the betrayal causes Simon to realize what he has done. He faces with a 'Why?' the attendant who strikes him.'' He is hung on the cross, where he prays that his persecutors be forgiven.

Jesus is most clearly defined in his passion, death and resurrection, and he simultaneously redefines what it is to be human. On the cross, Jesus is oppressed by others and isolated, and yet it is here that he is most visible, for he persists in his faithfulness to God and neighbor. At the same time, he redirects humanity because he reaches out to all men and women, accepting their rejection of him and hence their selfishness. The people display their inhumanity in the open toward Jesus, where some of them recognize it and seek God's forgiveness. Van Beeck writes: ''The rejected one does not reject. . . . Yet precisely because Jesus does not cease to relate to [others], they cannot help but respond: their very rejection of Jesus becomes an implicit testimony to the defectiveness of their own humanity and to the fullness of his.''[43]

Jesus' resurrection dispels any ambiguity about the identity of Jesus and his significance for all people. He is the one person who has remained faithful to God and neighbor, thereby drawing all people into a new relationship with God. To quote van Beeck:

Only ''this man Jesus,'' abandoned and rejected by all, and nobody else is affirmed and confirmed and placed in glory by the Father. He is the one and only person who kept faith with the Father's kingdom. But though it is only this one person who is glorified, his glory does not exclude humanity at large. In fact, in Jesus all of humankind is raised in glory precisely because he kept himself related to it as he absorbed and out-suffered their total rejection of him.[44]

Van Beeck's literary analysis of the Synoptic story yields an identifying account of the Gospels' protagonist. He is the ''man for others'' and the ''man for God.'' He is ''[t]he rejected one [who] does not reject.''[45] This is a portrait that results from the Gospels' realism. The interaction between Jesus and his world, as depicted in the scriptural narrative, produces a distinctive image of this Jesus. How then does the Synoptic story function in *Christ Proclaimed?* It yields an identifying account of the risen Lord—an account that is the basis for further inquiry into the identity of Jesus Christ.

III.3 *Story in Systematic Inquiry*

In *Christ Proclaimed* van Beeck argues for a new view of Christology, one in which the thematic or theoretical statements are linked to the Church's witness to and worship of Jesus Christ. In the course of this argument van Beeck contributes to our understanding of the process by which we identify Jesus Christ, for he fashions an individuating account of Jesus Christ as the point of reference for his thematic reflection on the person of Jesus Christ. What is so striking about chapter eleven is that it displays how a literary interpretation on the one hand and an understanding of person as relation on the other can work together to interpret the Gospels.

The aim of chapter eleven is to answer a question that comes up when one reflects on the Gospels' portrayal of Jesus' persistence in love. The question is, "What is it that animates this man to stand so long-sufferingly firm in his kindly determination to welcome all that is human into his person . . . ?"[46] The Synoptic Gospels' answer, as van Beeck states, is that Jesus draws strength from God. There is something about Jesus' bond with God that enables him to reach out to others while they reject him. Clarification of this relationship requires the use of more thematic or conceptual discourse than was needed in the inquiry to this point. In light of the fact that literary analysis has characterized Jesus in terms of his "interpersonalness," van Beeck adopts the language of person as relation.

Developmental psychology and humanistic philosophy have highlighted the relatedness of personal existence. Abraham Maslow, Carl Rogers and Martin Buber have shown, notes van Beeck, that we become persons through our encounters with and commitments to other persons. "False identity" is sought by asserting ourselves against others, and "authentic identity" unfolds as we give to and receive from others. Therefore, to be person is to be related to other persons. In van Beeck's words, "[Being-related] is an *entire* person's *modus* of being in such a way that the person is a self in the act or attitude of encounter.''[47] While our attitude toward others is often "I-it," that which is essential to us, the self, develops as we enter into "I-Thou" relationships.

When this notion of person is brought to a literary rendering of the Gospels, a number of things occur. First, it sheds light on the bond between Jesus Christ and God. To put it negatively, person as relation overturns a persistent misunderstanding. There is a tendency, says van Beeck, to speak of Jesus as though he possessed some divine "inner core" that enabled him to do what he did. This view does not hold up when it is tested against the Gospels where Jesus is presented as a human being involved in the giving and receiving of ordinary life. To state this positively, when person as relation is brought to our reflections on the source of Jesus' faithfulness, it displays the relationality that characterizes both Jesus Christ and God. It shows, observes van Beeck, that Jesus' "*modus* of being a person is one of absolute relatedness to the Father."[48]

Second, person as relation illuminates the relationship between Jesus Christ and the human community. Often we hold the misconception that the humanity of Jesus Christ is something added on to him. It is the means by which God's grace is introduced into creation. This view can be corrected by seeing that our own distinctive giving to and receiving from others is a gift. Our relating to others is indeed a gift from God that we share with others in our particular way. When we extend this idea to the Synoptic story, we see that Jesus' giving and receiving belongs to him alone, and it is universal. Jesus is defined by his interacting as a man with other men and women. Moreover, he relates to everyone, even to those who reject him. Hence, van Beeck states: "As a human person, Jesus is total gift; by actualizing beyond all human power human nature's native potential for total surrender and receptivity in relationship to God, he also actualizes human nature's native yet unheard-of potential for total self-giving and total openness to others."[49]

Third, when person as relation is brought to the Gospels, this notion itself is enriched. In strictly humanistic thought, person as relation says nothing explicit about our relationship to God. When understood in the light of the story of Jesus Christ, though, person as relation is changed so that it encompasses the relationship between God and us, and indeed sets this relationship at the heart of personal existence. Van Beeck states: "Jesus, therefore, is the revelation of human nature's dormant possibility to exist as the person of the Word of God.''[50] In other words: ''In the man Jesus, we see humanity re-created by total relatedness to God.''

Much more could be said about van Beeck's thematic reflection on the identity of Jesus Christ. We have not treated, for example, how this discussion of Jesus Christ as one who relates perfectly to God and humankind affords a new understanding of the language of Jesus Christ as the Logos. This is central to van Beeck's discursive account of the identity of Jesus, and it culminates in van Beeck's characterization of Jesus Christ as the ''Lamb slain from the beginning.''[51] Yet, our brief review of some aspects of van Beeck's thematic account suffices, for it displays one of the ways *Christ Proclaimed* contributes to our understanding of the process by which we answer ''Who is Jesus Christ?'' This work demonstrates how a notion of person, indeed a theory of personal existence, can help us interpret the Gospels, and also how the Gospels can shape our use of this notion.

Van Beeck has shown therefore that story and theory can complement one another in a systematic investigation of Jesus Christ. Christology can employ stories without being reduced to storytelling. Moreover, Christology can treat the Gospels as stories. It need not misconstrue these aesthetic units as expressions of a universal principle already known to us. Theory is enriched when it respects the independent status of a story, especially a realistic story, and allows a story to show the insufficiency of the theory. In a word, van Beeck has improved our skills in saying who Jesus Christ is because he has achieved the goal of his book. He has shown that Christology is a speech-act, consisting of both figurative and thematic discourse.

IV. *Story in a Reciprocal Method*

Van Beeck's *Christ Proclaimed* and Walter Kasper's *Jesus the Christ* have much in common. They both are oriented to the risen Christ, and hence the kerygma, as Christology's primary norm and point of departure. Moreover, both draw on three chief sources for our understanding of Jesus Christ: history, Scripture and tradition, and today's Church. For this reason, neither van Beeck nor Kasper would be satisfied with Barth's emphasis on one source alone, Scripture. Also, van Beeck and

Kasper agree that Christology concerns both the historical Jesus and the risen Christ. They differ however in the concrete way each proceeds. In fact, van Beeck relies heavily on two sources, tradition and contemporary thought, while Kasper depends on historical reconstruction as well as Scripture, tradition and the Church today. In light of this difference, a question emerges: How might a reciprocal method like Kasper's benefit from using story as van Beeck has?

As we saw in Chapter Two, in a Christology of reciprocity, historical research and the analysis of Scripture and tradition stand side by side. While this method's starting point is the Church's testimony that Jesus is the Christ, the results of historical-critical study claim an independent status. These findings are then positioned beside the believing community's teachings about Jesus Christ. Given this arrangement, we can envision an investigation in which an historical narrative about Jesus is recounted as well as the Gospels. These two recollections would then produce images of Jesus Christ that would converge to display different dimensions of this person.

To some extent, this kind of interplay between historical reconstruction and faith testimony already occurs in Kasper's *Jesus the Christ*. "The History and Destiny of Jesus Christ" and "The Mystery of Jesus Christ" are distinct, complementary sections of the book. The first section describes Jesus of Nazareth as an individual of "unparalleled originality," and the second presents the risen Christ as "the mediator between God and man."[52] These representations of Jesus complement one another. The historical figure, Jesus, who is identified with the kingdom of God, is the same person who is united completely with God and simultaneously with the human community as to reconcile God and creation. Implicit in this account are narratives about Jesus that, if made explicit, would produce even stronger images of Jesus Christ and therefore provide the basis for an even fuller identification of him.

One question that comes up when we bring together an historical narrative and a retelling of the Gospels concerns Christology's third source, the contemporary Church's life and thought. If a Christology of reciprocity would adopt more explicit narratives for two sources, could it also do so for its third source? Both van Beeck and Kasper critically employ recent ideas in their reflections on Christ. *Christ Proclaimed* incorporates humanistic philosophy and developmental psychology, and *Jesus the Christ* depends on a post-Enlightenment notion of freedom.

This reliance on a third source prompts the question: Is there a type of narrative that would convey the Christian assembly's encounter with Christ today?

The biography of an exemplary Christian could serve as the third source in a Christology of reciprocity.[53] In every age, there emerge men and women who embody some of the best ideas and concerns of their society and simultaneously live in such congruence with the Gospels that Christians informally acknowledge these individuals as saints. These persons' activities and very lives bear witness to Christ's presence in the world. A Christology of reciprocity could therefore include the life story of a saint—a narrative that would directly identify the saint and also indirectly identify Jesus Christ alive in the Spirit.

We can envision then a Christology of reciprocity in which each of the three sources is manifest in part in a narrative. A historical narrative about Jesus, the recounting of the Gospels and the biography of a modern saint would be brought together, and the confluence of their respective images would serve as the basis for a conceptual account of the identity of Jesus Christ. It would be possible, for instance, to juxtapose these three narratives: a retelling of the Gospel according to Mark, an historical narrative about Jesus, and a biographical review of Dorothy Day's life. These would offer distinct, complementary representations of Jesus Christ that would enrich a systematic inquiry into this singular reality. These are the sources I shall use in the next chapter's exercise.

In this chapter, we have seen one use of the Gospels in Christology. *Christ Proclaimed* displays how Matthew, Mark and Luke contribute to the Christian community's worship and service, and, beyond this, how they can serve as the basis for saying who Jesus Christ is. In van Beeck's hands, the Synoptic story functions as an identifying description of Jesus Christ. Now we can consider my proposal that what van Beeck has accomplished in a kerygmatic Christology is also possible within a Christology of reciprocity.

NOTES

1. Cf. Stephen Sykes, *The Identity of Christianity* (Philadelphia: Westminster, 1984); *idem,* "Story and Eucharist," *Interpretation,* XXXVII (October 1983), 365–376; Mary Collins and David Power (eds.), *Liturgy* (New York: Sea-

bury, 1983); Ronald F. Thiemann, "Piety, Narrative, and Christian Identity," *Word and World*, III (Spring 1983), 148–159; Mark Searle, "The Narrative Quality of Christian Liturgy," *Chicago Studies*, XXI (1982), 73–84.

2. Cf. Robert W. Funk, *The Poetics of Biblical Narrative* (Philadelphia: Fortress, 1986); Edgar V. McKnight, *The Bible and the Reader* (Philadelphia: Fortress Press, 1985); Raymond F. Collins, *Introduction to the New Testament* (Garden City: Doubleday, 1983), pp. 231–271; John Dominic Crossan, *Cliffs of Fall* (New York: Seabury 1980); Daniel Patte, *Structural Exegesis* (Philadelphia: Fortress, 1978); Norman R. Petersen, *Literary Criticism for the New Testament* (Philadelphia: Fortress, 1978); James Barr, *The Bible in the Modern World* (New York: Harper and Row, 1973), pp. 53–74; Amos Wilder, *The Language of the Gospel* (New York: Harper and Row, 1964).

3. Klemens Richter, *Liturgie—ein vergessenes Thema der Theologie?* (Freiburg: Herder, 1986); Geoffry Wainwright, *Doxology* (New York: Oxford University Press, 1980); John McIntyre, *The Shape of Christology* (Philadelphia: The Westminster Press, 1966), pp. 44–47.

4. Frans Jozef van Beeck, *Christ Proclaimed* (New York: Paulist, 1979), p. 115. This view of Christology in relation to confession is also conveyed in some of van Beeck's other writings: *idem, Catholic Identity After Vatican II* (Chicago: Loyola University Press, 1985); *idem*, "Professing the Uniqueness of Christ," *Chicago Studies*, XXIV (April 1985), 17–35; *idem*, "Christology," in: *The New Catholic Encyclopedia*, XVI (Washington, D.C.: McGraw-Hill, 1974), pp. 84–85.

5. For helpful discussions of *Christ Proclaimed*, see: Leander Keck, *A Future for the Historical Jesus*, revised edition (Philadelphia: Fortress, 1981), pp. 271–273; Brian McDermott, "Roman Catholic Christology," *Theological Studies*, XLI (1980), 339–367; Leon Renwart, "Un signe en butte à la contradiction," *Nouvelle revue théologique*, CII (1980), 716–755; in response to Renwart, see: Frans Jozef van Beeck, "Un seul Christ, plusiers confessions. Réponse au Père Renwart," *Nouvelle revue théologique*, CIV (1983), 384–396.

6. Van Beeck, *Christ Proclaimed*, pp. 52–53, 210–211, 226, 361.

7. *Ibid.*, p. 115. As Keck has noted, with its stress on presence *Christ Proclaimed* is similar to Peter C. Hodgson, *Jesus' Word and Presence* (Philadelphia: Fortress Press, 1971). Walter Kasper, *Jesus the Christ*, trans. V. Green (New York: Paulist Press, 1976), pp. 35–36.

8. Another narrative Christology is Dietrich Ritschl, *Memory and Hope* (New York: Macmillan, 1967); *idem, "Story" als Rohmaterial der Theologie* (Munich: Chr. Kaiser, 1976).

9. William H. Poteat, "Myths, Stories, History, Eschatology and Ac-

tion,'' in: Thomas Langford and W. Poteat (eds.), *Intellect and Hope* (Durham: Duke University Press, 1968), pp. 198–231, 226.

10. Van Beeck, *Christ Proclaimed,* p. 327.

11. *Ibid.,* p. 348.

12. *Ibid.,* p. 345.

13. *Ibid.,* pp. 327, 350.

14. *Ibid.,* p. 345.

15. Robert Alter, *The Art of Biblical Narrative* (New York: Basic Books, 1981); Erich Auerbach, *Mimesis,* trans. W. Trask (Princeton: Princeton University Press, 1968).

16. Van Beeck, *Christ Proclaimed,* p. 361.

17. Hans W. Frei, *The Eclipse of Biblical Narrative* (New Haven: Yale University Press, 1974); *idem, The Identity of Jesus Christ* (Philadelphia: Fortress Press, 1975). David H. Kelsey, *The Uses of Scripture in Recent Theology* (Philadelphia: Fortress, 1975); cf. *idem,* ''The Bible and Christian Theology,'' *The Journal of the American Academy of Religion,* XLVIII (1980), 386–402. Cf. William Placher, *The Thomist,* XL (1985), 392–416.

18. Frei, *The Eclipse of Biblical Narrative,* p. 10. Cf. Anthony C. Yu, ''Recovering the Sense of the Story,'' *The Journal of Religion,* LVIII (1978), 198–203.

19. Auerbach, *Mimesis,* p. 491.

20. Kelsey, *The Uses of Scripture in Recent Theology,* p. 39.

21. *Ibid.*

22. Frei, *The Identity of Jesus Christ,* p. xiv; cf. *idem,* ''The 'Literal Reading' of Biblical Narrative in the Christian Tradition: Does It Stretch or Will It Break?'' in: Frank McConnell (ed.), *The Bible and the Narrative Tradition* (New York: Oxford University Press, 1986), pp. 36–77.

23. George Lindbeck, ''The Bible as Realistic Narrative,'' in: Leonard Swidler (ed.), *Consensus in Theology?* (Philadelphia: The Westminster Press, 1980), pp. 81–85, 84.

24. Kelsey, *The Uses of Scripture in Recent Theology,* p. 47.

25. Frei, *The Eclipse of Biblical Narrative,* pp. 10–16.

26. Auerbach, *Mimesis,* p. 15.

27. Frei, *The Eclipse of Biblical Narrative,* pp. 12–13.

28. *Ibid.,* p. 10.

29. Karl Barth, *Church Dogmatics,* IV/2, ed. G. W. Bromiley and T. F. Torrance (Edinburgh: T. & T. Clark, 1958), pp. 154–163.

30. Kelsey, *The Uses of Scripture in Recent Theology,* p. 48.

31. van Beeck, *Christ Proclaimed,* p. 238.

32. *Ibid.,* p. 94.

33. *Ibid.*, p. 520.

34. *Ibid.*, p. 327.

35. Cf. John R. Searle, *Speech-Acts* (London: Cambridge University Press, 1969).

36. van Beeck, *Christ Proclaimed*, p. 93.

37. *Ibid.*, 108.

38. *Ibid.*, 326.

39. *Ibid.*, p. 363.

40. *Idem.*

41. *Ibid.*, p. 364.

42. *Ibid.*, p. 366.

43. *Ibid.*, p. 367.

44. *Ibid.*, p. 368.

45. *Ibid.*, p. 367.

46. *Ibid.*, pp. 375, 418.

47. *Ibid.*, p. 409.

48. *Ibid.*, p. 423.

49. *Ibid.*, p. 445.

50. *Ibid.*, p. 447.

51. *Ibid.*, p. 400.

52. Kasper, *Jesus the Christ*, pp. 65, 230.

53. Johann Baptist Metz is one proponent of biography in theology. Cf. J.B. Metz, "An Identity Crisis in Christianity," in: William Kelly (ed.), *Theology and Discovery* (Milwaukee: Marquette University Press, 1980), pp. 169–178, 171; *idem, Faith in History and Society,* trans. D. Smith (New York: The Seabury Press, 1980), pp. 209–210; *idem, Followers of Christ,* trans. T. Linton (New York: Paulist Press, 1978), p. 40. Cf. Francis Schüssler Fiorenza, "Fundamental Theology and the Enlightenment," *The Journal of Religion,* LXII (July 1982), 289–298.

Chapter Five

THREE NARRATIVES IN CHRISTOLOGY

Christology is the disciplined inquiry into the question: Who is Jesus Christ? It aims at identifying the person whom Christians confess as the Lord, as the Son of God. One form of this investigation is what Walter Kasper calls a Christology of reciprocity, a Christology that integrates research about the historical Jesus and critical reflection on the risen Christ. Kasper has undertaken this Christology of complementarity in his *Jesus the Christ* with impressive results. This kind of study would be even stronger, however, if its inherent narratives were more explicit. If narratives about Jesus and his followers were actually retold within the systematic investigation, they would clarify the meaning of the inquiry's discursive statements about Jesus Christ. I shall demonstrate this claim.

The question "Who is Jesus Christ?" cannot be adequately pursued in a few pages. It can however be narrowed down so that its answer stays within the bounds of a chapter. John Paul II struck a deep chord among Christians when, in *Redemptor Hominis,* he described the Church as "the community of disciples."[1] This image is so rich and timely that Avery Dulles adopted it in order to convey one "vision" of Church for the 1980's.[2] I too will use it to focus the primary Christological question. Thus, instead of asking "Who is Jesus Christ?" let us ask: "Who is Lord of the community of disciples? Who is the person whom the community of disciples call the Christ?" This way of putting the identity question limits the scope of our inquiry. Moreover, it clearly locates the question within the Christian assembly—the location which, as Kasper, Edward Schillebeeckx and Frans Jozef van Beeck agree, has the sources for a full response to the issue of Jesus' identity.

The primary sources for our inquiry are three narratives. The first of these is Mark's Gospel, a call to discipleship. It functions here in a way comparable to both the scriptural texts in Kasper's reflection on the mystery of Christ in *Jesus the Christ* and the "Synoptic story" in van Beeck's *Christ Proclaimed*. Our inquiry's second source is an historical narrative about Jesus of Nazareth. This is similar to Kasper's historical reconstruction as well as to Schillebeeckx's "post-critical narrative history" in *Jesus*. Finally, our third source is the life story of a modern disciple, Dorothy Day.[3] This provides a contemporary source like Kasper's reliance on the idea of freedom and van Beeck's use of developmental psychology. Mark's Gospel, an historical review of Jesus' ministry, suffering and death, and a biographical sketch of Dorothy Day are briefly retold in the first part of our effort to answer: "Who is Jesus Christ?"

Reflection on these three narratives constitutes the second part of this investigation. While the three narratives *show* who Jesus is, critical reflection *says* who he is. It identifies Jesus Christ in figurative terms and then in more conceptual discourse. That is, the retelling of Mark's Gospel, an historical narrative about Jesus, and Dorothy Day's life produce the image of Jesus Christ as the founder of the new people of compassion. He is the person in whom human aspirations have been united and directed toward their final goal, God. We need not stop here, for we can also adopt the language of self-agency. This founder is God's agent. Jesus Christ is the one who has enacted both God's longing to bring creation to the fullness of life and also humankind's yearning to live for the glory of God. Straightforward statements of this sort conclude our inquiry into the identity of Jesus Christ—an investigation that began with narratives.

This inquiry is not an entire Christology. If it were, its initial question would be broader. We would ask not simply "Who is the community's Lord?" but instead "Who is Jesus Christ?" Moreover, if our endeavor were complete, we would take more than narratives from Scripture and tradition, historical research and contemporary thought. We would treat, for example, the classic formulations of the Christological councils. Also, we would pursue relevant issues of philosophy and theology. Rather, I have presented solely an exercise that demonstrates how narratives about Jesus can enhance a systematic inquiry. It is motivated by the conviction that some types of narratives allow us to know dimensions of personal existence which would elude us if we excluded narratives from our discourse. Once we have finished this exercise, we can consider, in the final chapter, the conviction regarding the cognitive value of narratives.

I.1 *Jesus Christ, the Inaugurator of the Kingdom*

Who is the person whom the community of disciples calls the Christ? Our first source for an answer is Scripture, specifically Mark's Gospel, the Gospel that emphasizes discipleship.[4] According to Mark, Jesus Christ is "the Son of God" (1:1). He is the one whom God calls "my beloved Son" at his baptism (1:11) and transfiguration (9:7), and who is acknowledged as "the Son of God" by "the unclean spirits" (3:11; cf. 5:7), the high priest (14:62), and the centurion at the cross (15:39).

By itself, "the Son of God" tells us very little, for it takes its meaning from the narrative within which it functions. Mark's story needs therefore to be retold, though at the outset we can give a summary statement. In this drama, Jesus Christ is the inaugurator of God's rule. He is the vineyard owner's son who, after other emissaries failed, came to the vineyard and was put to death by the wicked husbandmen, thereby ushering in the day when the owner would reclaim the land (12:1–12).

As the story opens, the world has reached its crucial juncture. John the Baptizer stands as the last in the line of God's prophets, for example, of Moses and Elijah (9:5). Now John declares the advent of the special herald whose appearance will ignite the decisive conflict in the cosmic struggle between God and Satan. The signs of this showdown are evident to some Jews, and these people receive John's baptism of repentance on the banks of the Jordan River.

Jesus steps out of the crowd. He too undergoes John's baptism, and, as he is lifted out of the water, he hears a voice from heaven declare, "Thou art my beloved Son" (1:11). Jesus goes into the desert, and he does not succumb to Satan's seductions. Satan withdraws to bide his time. With the arrest of John, Jesus takes up the ministry in Galilee, proclaiming, "The time is fulfilled, and the kingdom of God is at hand; repent and believe the Gospel" (1:15).

Jesus announces the breaking in of God's reign. He cures Peter's mother-in-law; he heals the daughter of a pagan, the Syrophoenician woman (7:25). In Capernaum's synagogue Jesus exorcises a man. On the sabbath he forgives the sins of a paralytic and also restores his health, insisting: "The sabbath was made for man, not man for the sabbath" (2:27). He calms the storm-tossed waters of Galilee. In such parables as the sower and also the mustard seed he teaches about this new order. He eats with a mixed group, and then later, in a deserted place, he dines again with a large crowd and a few loaves and fish. Jesus selects disciples, for example, Peter and Andrew, and James and John, so that others may aid in the coming of God's kingdom.

Jesus does not fit with the groups around him. He teaches, for instance, with authority (1:22). Pharisees and Herodians, suspicious of Jesus, join forces and plot against him (3:6). His family is convinced, "He is beside himself" (3:21). His disciples do not comprehend him. John the Baptizer is beheaded. Tension mounts around Jesus.

Time and again, Jesus' true identity is sought. As Jesus expels a demon, the demon exclaims: "I know who you are, the Holy One of God" (1:24). After Jesus stills the storm, his disciples wonder, "Who then is this, that even wind and sea obey him" (4:41). Jesus' townsfolk ask, "Is not this the carpenter, the son of Mary . . . ?" (6:3). Herod too wonders about Jesus, and surmises: "John, whom I beheaded, has been raised" (6:16).

At Caesarea Philippi, the disciples discuss all of this with Jesus who questions them about how others perceive him. Then Jesus leads Peter to confess, "You are the Christ" (8:29). Jesus clarifies that he is indeed the "Son of man" who must suffer and be put to death for the new kingdom to arrive. Shortly afterward, in the company of Peter, James and John, Jesus is "transfigured," and God reiterates the message of Jesus' baptism: "This is my beloved Son" (9:7).

From this point on, with a new urgency, Jesus turns his attention to his disciples. He instructs them on their life of service for the kingdom. They are confused and fearful when Jesus sets off to Jerusalem (10:32). At the sacred city, Jesus provokes a confrontation. He allows the people to greet him as a king. He cleanses the temple. When challenged by the authorities, he tells the parable of the wicked husbandmen (12:1–12), infuriating his listeners. He announces Jerusalem's imminent end. Then he celebrates the meal of the new kingdom with his followers and withdraws to pray.

After anguishing in prayer, Jesus no longer takes the initiative. He submits to the temple guard. Led before the Sanhedrin, Jesus is asked if he is "the Christ, the Son of the Blessed" (14:61). "I am," says Jesus. He is taken to Pilate who inquires, "Are you the King of the Jews?" "You have said so," answers the carpenter's son. Then the soldiers scourge Jesus, force him to bear his timber to Golgotha, and nail him to the cross upon which he dies. A centurion looks on and declares, "Truly, this man was the Son of God" (15:39).

Jesus is buried by his followers. After three days, his tomb is visited by Mary Magdalene, Mary the mother of James, and Salome. They find it empty and are told by "a young man": "He is risen . . . he is going before you to Galilee . . . " (16:6–7). The three women flee in fear.

What happens next in the conflict between God and Satan? Is Jesus indeed the Son of God, and, if so, is he also "the Son of man sitting at the right hand of Power, and coming with the clouds of heaven" (14:62)? As in the parable of the wicked husbandmen, this Son's death has brought an end to the old order, but the new kingdom that the Son preached has not yet arrived. When it does, Jesus will return. This abrupt, open-ending brings about two responses.

First, the logic of the story calls for a happy ending.[5] From the outset, when Jesus is baptized and blessed by God, the drama conveys the sense that all will end well. Jesus will draw Satan from his lair and be killed, but ironically Satan will undo himself in the act of destroying Jesus (3:26). Jesus will be victorious; he will be exalted and return in the future (8:38; 9:32; 10:34). Hence, the Gospel promotes an appearance story of the sort now appended to it: Jesus "rose" from the dead and appears to Mary Magdalene, to two disciples in the country, and to the eleven. Then he is "taken up into heaven," from where he works with the disciples for the coming of the kingdom (16:9–20). Whereas the parable of the wicked husbandmen ends with the son's death, Mark's Gospel opens to the Son's exaltation and return in glory.[6]

Second, the Gospel prompts today's readers to ask two questions. On the one hand, it raises the issue: Who was Jesus of Nazareth? Mark's account of Jesus Christ invites us to review the ministry of the historical figure who gave rise to this testimony. Such a study is meant not to reduce the Gospel's meaning to that of an historical reconstruction, but to set the distinct representations side by side. On the other hand, retelling the Gospel can move us to ask: Who is Jesus Christ today, as known through those who have lived as his disciples? Mark's account directs us to recall the witness of modern women and men who have lived the kind of lives to which the Gospel calls its readers. Each of these questions results in a narrative about Jesus.

I.2 *Jesus, Teacher of God's Kingdom*

While we do not know enough about Jesus' life and times to write his biography, we do have today a consensus among many historians and exegetes about important details of Jesus' ministry.[7] This data need not be merely listed, it can be arranged in such a way as to form an historical narrative about Jesus—a narrative that, without distorting the facts, produces one possible image of Jesus. In *Jesus* Schillebeeckx has fashioned such an account that portrays Jesus as "the latter-day prophet." Let us also turn to an historical narrative, told in response to our initial question about the disciples' Lord and in light of Mark's Gospel.

Who was Jesus of Nazareth? He was a Jewish religious teacher in Palestine, put to death by Jewish and Roman authorities in approximately 30 C.E. He was regarded by some of his followers as the herald of the last days before God's transformation of the world. There were however other images of him. This Jesus was also judged, for instance, by some of the legitimate authorities as a trouble-maker.

Jesus was born at the end of the reign of Herod the Great (37–4 B.C.E.). His parents were Joseph, a carpenter, and Mary. He grew up in Nazareth of Galilee, a region in which some people converted to Jewish belief only one hundred and twenty-five years before his birth.[8] Moreover, Galilee gave birth to such charismatic preachers as Honi the Circle-Drawer, before Jesus, and Hanina ben Dosa, after Jesus.[9] Both of these men were persecuted when they attempted to teach in Jerusalem.

In approximately 28 C.E., Jesus was immersed in the Jordan River by John the Baptizer, thereby undergoing the ritual of repentance in expectation of God's judgment in human affairs. This purification rite may have originated with the Essenes, a Jewish sect at Qumran on the Dead Sea. Moreover, it indicates that Jesus, along with some of his contemporaries, anticipated a major change, an apocalyptic event, erupting in his day. Sometime after his baptism, Jesus began to teach a message similar to John's: he declared that the end-time was near. Jesus differed though from John in that he stressed God's love whereas John had emphasized God's judgment. John was arrested by Herod Antipas, the tetrarch of Galilee and Perea, and eventually executed. Jesus continued to teach throughout Galilee, especially in and around Capernaum.

Jesus proclaimed the coming of "the kingdom of God," alluding to the theme of "the day of the Lord" (Am 5:18–20; Is 11:6). Jesus' message concerned God's new and decisive offer of compassion, especially to the poor, the sick, the ritually impure, and the outcasts, for example, prostitutes. To express this insight Jesus told parables, for example, the lost sheep (Lk 15:1–7), the great supper (Mt 22:1–4), and the sower (Mt 13:3–8).[10]

God is making this healing offer, declared Jesus, in the present, and God would bring it to fulfillment in the future. Thus, Jesus spoke with a sense of urgency. Also, he presented his message with an unusual self-confidence. He did not appeal to rabbinical precedents in the same way as many teachers, but spoke on his own authority, as exhibited in his use of "Amen." Moreover, Jesus implicitly linked the coming of God's reign with himself as the final prophet.

To spread his message Jesus gathered disciples, apart from John's followers. Unlike most of the rabbis, who waited for students to come to them, Jesus took the initiative and picked some people to receive special instruction. He enjoined his followers to live by radical demands for welcoming God's new rule—demands that were by-and-large more rigorous than those made by other teachers. This is evident, for example, in the sayings that later developed into the Sermon on the Mount. Further, Jesus addressed God as Abba in private prayer—a rare practice for Jews of the day—and he taught his disciples also to address God as "Daddy."[11] At some point, Jesus selected "the twelve" to lead his followers. These included Simon bar Jonah, Simon's brother Andrew, James and John (the sons of Zebedee), and Judas Iscariot. Jesus' choice of twelve symbolized God's imminent restoration of Israel.

Jesus taught his message not only in his words but also in his deeds. He dined with a wide range of people, including tax collectors, Pharisees, women, and the poor. He cured some people of their ailments and exorcised others, and on occasion he even performed these mighty works for Gentiles. Some of Jesus' behavior caused controversy: for instance, he healed on the sabbath and forgave sins without demanding repentance. In these instances, as in others, Jesus' actions were meant to corroborate his teaching about God's reign: the afflicted hear good news, the brokenhearted are healed, captives and prisoners are set free, and the grieving are comforted, for this is the time of God's favor (Is 61:1–2; cf. Lk 4:17–19).

During Jesus' ministry, opposition to him grew. In Nazareth, some people averred that Jesus was not mentally stable (Mk 3:21). The Jewish authorities were charged with ridding their people of false teachers and pseudo-messiahs (Dt 18:20–22), and some of these leaders took note of Jesus' conduct, for example, his implicit claim to be the final prophet.[12] Also, in Jerusalem members of the priestly aristocracy were alerted to this Nazarean when he criticized temple practices (Mk 13).

These tensions peaked during Jesus' last stay in Jerusalem. As preparations for Passover were underway, Jesus arrived and attracted a crowd, so that a procession occurred. Then Jesus "cleansed" the temple area for God's approaching restoration of Israel. Anticipating a confrontation with the authorities, Jesus celebrated a farewell meal with his followers. At this time, Jesus conveyed the sense that his mission included his suffering, death and eventual vindication. Afterward, he withdrew to Gethsemane to pray.

The temple leaders and the Roman authorities wanted to curtail any turmoil in the city during the celebration of major pilgrimage feasts. Therefore, aided by Judas Iscariot, they arrested Jesus. Jesus' followers scattered, and Peter denied any ties with the Nazarean. Some members of the Sanhedrin held a hearing about Jesus' disruptive behavior and then turned him over to Pontius Pilate. The Roman prefect of Judea judged Jesus guilty of sedition and sentenced him to death. Before the eve of Passover, Jesus was crucified, with the inscription "The King of the Jews" affixed to the cross. After his death, Jesus was buried by the few followers who had not fled.

Sometime after his death, talk sprang up about Jesus. One tradition declares that some women found Jesus' tomb empty (Mk 16:1–8). Another tradition tells that Jesus "appeared" to some of his followers and then was "taken up" to God's side (Mk 16:9–20). Believing in Jesus as the exalted, anointed one, communities of followers formed to pray, care for one another, and proclaim the "good news" of Jesus "the Christ" as they awaited his return (Rev 22:20) when God would establish the new kingdom.

Who then was Jesus of Nazareth? He was a charismatic Jewish teacher who, at approximately age thirty-five, was crucified outside the walls of Jerusalem during the reign of Tiberius Caesar. He died preaching the coming of God's kingdom.

I.3 *Jesus Christ, According to Dorothy Day's Witness*

Our recollecting of Mark's Gospel has yielded a portrait of Jesus as "the Son of God," as the inaugurator of God's reign in history. Our historical narrative of Jesus' ministry has depicted Jesus as a teacher of God's new order. These two separate, yet complementary depictions of Jesus prompt us to look for a modern characterization of Jesus Christ that fills out our theme of discipleship. One such image is conveyed by the witness of Dorothy Day. Our question therefore is: "Who is Jesus Christ, as attested to by Dorothy Day?" We can answer this by recounting Day's life.

In the preface to her autobiography, *The Long Loneliness,* Day says that her life divides into two periods.[13] The first encompasses approximately her first thirty years. Born on November 8, 1897, in Brooklyn, Dorothy moved with her family to Oakland, California when she was a few months old. Her father, a nominal Episcopalian, worked as a newspaper reporter. On April 18, 1906, the earthquake destroyed the newspaper and the Days' home so that the family relocated in Chicago. For the next five years, the Days lived in poverty as Mr. Day attempted to write a novel. When nothing came of this, he again took a job as a reporter. The family's standard of living gradually improved, but Dorothy could not forget the poverty. As a teenager, she read Upton Sinclair's novels and took her brother for walks in rundown neighborhoods.

In 1913 Dorothy Day received a scholarship to the University of Illinois. Haunted by loneliness and committed to the activities of socialist groups on campus, Day lost interest in her formal studies. In 1915 she dropped out of school and moved to New York City, following her family. Residing in a boarding house, she barely survived as a reporter for the socialist newspaper, *The Masses.* Then, Day fell in love with the journalist, Lionel Moise. When she became pregnant, she underwent an abortion rather than lose Moise. When he moved to Chicago in 1919, Day did too. A year later, the affair abruptly ended; Day returned to New York. With $5,000 she received from the movie rights to her novel *The Eleventh Virgin,* Day eventually purchased a cottage on Staten Island.

For the next seven years, she lived on the beach with her common-law husband, Forster Batterham, an atheist biologist.

The second part of Day's life began when, in 1927 at the age of thirty, she gave birth to her daughter, Tamar. This event crystallized Day's conviction that in her life near the ocean she had discovered God. Now she wanted her daughter to grow up with an explicit religious training. Thus, she had Tamar baptized in the Catholic Church, and then a few months later Day herself was baptized. Abandoned by Batterham and socialist friends, Day began writing for *Commonweal*. In 1932, George Shuster, then the managing editor of the Catholic periodical, introduced Day to Peter Maurin, an itinerant French philosopher-peasant with a vision for a new social order based on the Gospels. Day and Maurin worked together for the poor.

To realize Maurin's dream, in 1933 Day and Maurin opened a soup kitchen in lower Manhattan. Simultaneously, they published their first issue of *The Catholic Worker*. Soon the Catholic Worker Movement spread. Other men and women joined Day and Maurin in feeding and housing the poor and in speaking out for justice and Christian pacifism. In 1947 Maurin died; however Day and the Movement persisted.[14]

By the time of her death on November 29, 1980, Day had founded more than forty houses of hospitality throughout the United States and Canada. Under her guidance, the Movement has stayed within the Catholic Church. This bond did not however keep Day from criticizing the Church when she judged that justice was at stake. For example, in 1949 she supported New York City's gravediggers against Francis Cardinal Spellman. Moreover, Day was an ardent pacifist. Her non-violent demonstrations for peace and also for workers' rights led to her arrest on more than a dozen occasions.

This is the life of a Christian disciple, of a woman committed to the risen Lord. With her conversion in her late twenties, Day dedicated her life to worshiping and serving God in union with Jesus Christ. For her, this entailed membership in the Catholic Church and living with the poor. Influenced by Fyodor Dostoevski's *The Brothers Karamazov* (1880), Karl Adam's *The Spirit of Catholicism* (1924), and Pius XII's *Mystici Corporis* (1943), she spoke of Jesus Christ as the head of "the mystical body." Since her sense of herself depended so greatly on her view of the "Lord," we can attain through her life one glimpse of the risen Christ today.

Dorothy Day was the founder of a movement, specifically of house-holds of hospitality. She knew homelessness and poverty from her child-hood years. This experience of loss resulted in her alienation from society at large. In late adolescence she realized that she did not want to live according to society's conventions. She set out to change things. After ten years, something did change—in Day. She converted to Ca-tholicism, and with her conversion she accepted her estrangement from society.[15] One manifestation of this is her acceptance of herself as a mother, though not a conventional mother. Along with cherishing her daughter, she embraced the homeless and the poor by establishing shel-ters for displaced persons. In a word, Day was the founder of an alter-native kind of household. As she states: "We felt a respect for the poor and destitute as those nearest to God, as those chosen by Christ for his compassion. Christ lived among men."[16]

Who is Jesus Christ, as reflected in Day's life? He is God's com-passionate presence and therefore the founder of the people of compas-sion.[17] He is the one whom Day herself encountered on the beach, enabling her to accept her daughter and her homelessness. Also, as she believed, this Lord called her to welcome others without homes and to speak for them through her journalism. In Day's view, Christ continued to meet her when she met cast-offs and refugees. As the founder of households of hospitality, Dorothy Day mirrored Jesus Christ, the foun-der of all communities of care.

II.1 Jesus Christ, The Founder

We have reviewed three distinct narratives: the Gospel according to Mark, an historical review of Jesus' ministry, and the life of Dorothy Day. While these accounts are dissimilar in their specific form and con-tent, they are linked in their reference to a single person, Jesus Christ. Moreover, various images of this person emerge from the three recol-lections, and one in particular can be developed here. I shall argue that the three narratives produce the view that *Jesus Christ is the founder of the new people of compassion.* To do this, I will elucidate the meaning of this statement's elements, that is, Jesus Christ as "the founder," then "the new people," and finally "compassion."

Consider first our ordinary sense of "founder." A founder is one who transforms and directs already existing tendencies, by means of personal example and a lasting vision. One example of a founder is Dorothy Day. Throughout the late 1920's and early 1930's, as the Great Depression worsened, many people realized that something needed to be done for those without jobs, food and homes. Under President Franklin Delano Roosevelt, the federal government did adopt assistance programs in late 1933. But what about those people who fell through the net? Here is where Day gathered others' resources and marshaled them to help people who may not otherwise receive it. Through her dedication to and life with the indigent, she demonstrated the kind of community she advocated. Others, drawn by her example, formed her households, and today they live out her vision without her. Such is the character of a founder, and this understanding can be extended to serve as one analogy for Jesus Christ.

God is the one and only Creator. According to Jewish monotheism, God is the sole source of life and its sustainer (Gen 1; Ex 3).[18] Yet, Christians confess that Jesus Christ stands at the heart of God's creation. This presence can be expressed in the image of founder. While God is the Creator, Jesus Christ is creation's founder, the one in whom, through the Holy Spirit, creation is transformed and directed toward its fulfillment in God. An image similar to this is that of "the firstborn" in the Letter to the Colossians:[19]

> He is the image of the invisible God, the first-born of all creation . . . all things were created through him and for him. He is before all things, and in him all things hold together. He is the head of the body, the Church; he is the beginning, the first-born from the dead, that in everything he might be preeminent. For in him all the fullness of God was pleased to dwell, and through him to reconcile to himself all things, whether on earth or in heaven, making peace by the blood of his cross (Col 1:15–20).

The image of Jesus Christ as founder, as well as that of "the firstborn," can be misconstrued to support talk about the importance of membership in the Church, to undergird exclusivism. This distortion need not, however, occur. In fact, when these images are kept in contact with scriptural testimony about Jesus Christ, they convey the sense of

God's universal love in Christ. By referring to our previous narratives, we can identify Jesus Christ as the founder of all creation.

In an historical perspective, Jesus is the founder of a religious community which eventually split off from Judaism.[20] Jesus drew a wide range of people into his table companionship, and he selected twelve disciples to symbolize God's imminent restoration of Israel—a new Israel fashioned of all peoples.[21] He instructed his followers in his message and introduced them to such rituals as the fellowship meal. Moreover, this founder shared with his followers the source of his inspiration, namely, his understanding of God as Abba. Finally, he foresaw his rejection by his contemporaries, viewing this as an integral part of his mission, and he looked forward to his vindication when the kingdom he proclaimed would be fully realized. According to our historical narrative, Jesus is one religious founder among others.

Mark's Gospel adds to our perception of Jesus as founder through its portrayal of the Son of God. The protagonist of this narrative is not one religious leader among others; he is the leader, indeed the inaugurator of God's reign.[22] As he is baptized by John, God declares that this Jesus is "my beloved Son" (Mk 1:11). God reiterates this, after the transfiguration, as Jesus' ministry moves toward its climax in Jerusalem. While God has called forth other founders, God has singled out this Jesus. He is *the* founder of God's people. He is the vineyard owner's true Son—the Son whose death does not unleash God's fury, but lavishes God's compassion, God's readiness to suffer so that human hearts and minds might be turned to God, as happens to the centurion, a Gentile, at the cross (Mk 15:39).

Dorothy Day is also a founder. Along with Peter Maurin, she founded the Catholic Worker movement. A biography about her directly reveals Day: her struggle, her sensitivity, her dedication, and her vision. Yet, it indirectly discloses the source of her inspiration: Jesus Christ, the "head of the mystical body."[23] The households Day established would reach out to all people, she believed, so long as their "workers" ordered their lives to Jesus Christ. Discipleship to this one person demands service for all people. Even more paradoxically, in Day's view commitment to Jesus Christ includes participation in a specific church, the Catholic Church, but this participation simultaneously directs one's attention outside that assembly so that one cares for neighbors, strangers and enemies without demanding that they acknowledge Jesus Christ or join one's church. According to Day's witness, anchoring one's life in Jesus Christ brings one into communion with the entire human family.

These three recollections identify a single person. He is the historical figure who lived from approximately 4 B.C.E. until 30 C.E. Also, he is the protagonist in a narrative edited by Mark in approximately 75 C.E. Further, he is the person, alive in God's Spirit, to whom Day and her followers have committed their lives with the result that they have given themselves indiscriminately to others. One image that unites these three distinct views is that Jesus Christ is the founder of the community to which all of creation is being drawn by God's Spirit. One person, Jesus Christ, is the point of union for God's new creation.

II.2 *The New People*

According to the Hebrew Scriptures, since the dawn of time God has called all of humankind to form into a single people, and God chose the people of Israel to become a sign of this future reality (Is 2:1–4).[24] The human family exists in God's covenant of love. Yet the peoples of the earth bear the mark of Cain (Gen 4:15). Discord and hate tear the threads that bind men and women into families, regions, nations and the human family. Nevertheless, union with God, neighbor and self for which all people yearn has already been realized in one person. The promise of solidarity has been fulfilled in Jesus Christ, as we can see by reflecting further upon our earlier narratives.

Historical inquiry highlights that Jesus did not preach himself, but God's kingdom. This new reality, declared Jesus, is breaking into history, and God is overturning the old state of affairs. Jesus preached this message in parables, for example, that of the mustard seed (Mk 4:30–32). He displayed it with his cures and table companionship. Further, he confirmed this order through his passion and death. The one thing worth living and dying for is God's new creation. Moreover, Jesus witnessed to the universal character of this community through his outreach to men and women of all stations in life and even to non-Jews, for example, the Syrophoenician woman. Jesus of Nazareth lived and died witnessing to God's election of all people.[25]

Mark's Gospel enriches this view of Jesus and God's universal election of all people. Those interested in Jesus' identity include both Jews and Gentiles.[26] For example, along with the townsfolk and religious leaders, even Herod Antipas (Mk 6:16) and Pilate (Mk 15:2) ask who Jesus is. Further, Jesus, the Son of God, relativizes temple practices and foresees a new bonding of people. He insists: "Is it not written, 'My house shall be called a house of prayer for all the nations'? But you have made it a den of robbers" (Mk 11:17). Further, upon Jesus' death the veil of the temple is rent; the old form, with its exclusivity, is torn asunder. Immediately afterward the centurion declares, "Truly this man was the Son of God" (Mk 15:39). This Gentile soldier stands as a symbol: all nations shall acknowledge Jesus as their Lord, the person in whom they are united.

Dorothy Day recognized the oneness of all people in union with Jesus Christ. On the one hand, she had no illusions about the human heart. She knew alienation through her own failings and her intense loneliness, as well as through social evil. She knew the disparity between what social agencies would promise and what they could in fact do for people. On the other hand, Day believed in the community of all men and women. She perceived that all peoples, no matter what their lot in life, are united with the risen Christ. Moreover, she discerned this communion where most of us dare not even look, namely among the dispossessed. Writes Day: "The Catholic Worker movement, working for a new social order, has come to be known as a community which breaks bread with brothers of whatever race, color or creed."[27] For Day, belief in one person, Jesus Christ, affords an astute confidence in all people.

Jesus Christ is the founder of a new people, indeed of *the* new people. While alienation and tribalism characterize human interaction, this state of affairs is no longer the norm. The unity of all nations has been secured through the ministry, death and resurrection of one person, Jesus. To cite St. Paul, humankind is no longer bound to the "old Adam," but has been united in the "new Adam" (1 Cor 15:45; Rom 5:14). No longer is the human family tied primarily to its past self; now all women and men are called to their future selves, already realized in Jesus Christ.

II.3 *The Compassionate Founder*

In the Bible, God's dealings with creation are marked by "covenantal love" (*hesed*).[28] God initiated the covenant with Israel, and God sustains it. Here is manifest God's "loving kindness." As written in the Decalogue, "You shall not make for yourself a graven image . . . for I the Lord your God am a jealous God . . . showing steadfast love to thousands of those who love me and keep my commandments" (Ex 20:4–6). Because of this benevolence, God goes beyond what can reasonably be expected in the covenant. God stands with the chosen people in their hardship and even in their unfaithfulness. God's steadfast love includes compassion, namely, sharing in another's anguish and seeking to alleviate it. This persistent, indeed identifying dynamism in God is embodied in Jesus Christ.

Jesus of Nazareth was a man of compassion.[29] He initiated faithful relationships with his disciples, as when he called Peter. He endured their misunderstanding and inconstancy, as when they refused to comprehend the inevitability of his suffering. Moreover, he healed people of physical and spiritual illnesses, as a sign of the coming reality he proclaimed. He welcomed the support of women such as Mary Magdalene, Mary the mother of James, and Salome, and he gained their trust. He recognized the fear and hate of his adversaries. He allowed himself to be taken by them, thereby becoming another victim of injustice. Yet, unlike other innocent victims, he did not curse his persecutors. He sought not revenge, but forgiveness.

Mark's Gospel illuminates Jesus' person and work through its emphasis on Jesus' suffering and death on the cross. Jesus is not only the Son of God, he is also the Son of man who must suffer for the sins of many.[30] He sets people free through his rejection: "The Son of man also came not to be served but to serve, and to give his life as a ransom for many" (Mk 10:45). He is the vineyard owner's son who surrenders to the tenants' oppression so that they might experience a change of heart and be freed from their evil. Thus, Jesus appears as the Suffering Servant, led like a lamb to slaughter (Is 53:7). He is the scapegoat driven into a deserted place to die abandoned. Yet through rejection and injustice hope emerges; the God whom the beloved Son called Abba has the last word. Out of defeat, God brings victory for Jesus and his followers. In this, God's compassion is manifest: the Son of God suffered the anguish of humankind, and through his resurrection he has alleviated this condition through hope.

Dorothy Day was a woman of compassion. She shared her table

with whoever walked in off the street. She listened to the people on society's margin and then spoke for them in *The Catholic Worker* and elsewhere. She eschewed all forms of manipulation through her espousal of pacifism. Whether challenging the archdiocese of New York or the United States government or the grape growers of California, she opted for becoming a victim along with the people whose poverty left them little choice but to be wronged. Paradoxically, her powerlessness became her power. By standing with the dispossessed and being hurt with them, she disclosed injustice, moved the hearts of some, and renewed the victims' hope. Day observes: "To go on picket lines to protest discrimination in housing, or to protest the draft, is one of the works of mercy, which include rebuking the sinner, enlightening the ignorant, counselling the doubtful."[31] In Day's view, when she stood with the poor, she shared in the sufferings of Christ and witnessed to the promise springing from Christ's passion, death and resurrection.

Our three sources identify Jesus Christ as the embodiment of God's covenantal love. Jesus Christ is the Savior. He has relinquished himself to manipulative, satanic powers, and through his weakness he has defused history's dark forces. Raised from death, the Christ stands at the heart of the human community as the new Adam to whom all people are drawn and united by God's Spirit. Thus, in each era God calls forth men and women to witness, as Dorothy Day has, to the mystery revealed in Jesus Christ. Indeed, Jesus Christ is the founder of the new people of compassion.

This reflection on the identity of Jesus Christ has arisen from our three narratives—an historical narrative about Jesus, Mark's Gospel, and a biography of Dorothy Day—and it has drawn out one image of Jesus Christ, namely, that he is the founder of the new people of compassion. This reflection need not however stop here, for it can shift from the use of figurative terms, for instance, "founder" and "people," to reliance on more conceptual words, for example, "personal agency," "relation," or "subjectivity." To be sure, such a change has disadvantages; for example, it relinquishes figurative speech's specificity. Nevertheless, it also possesses merits; for example, it gains thematic discourse's clarity, thereby shedding even further light on the reality of Jesus Christ. The language we shall adopt for this last phase of reflection is that of personal agency.

III.1 *Jesus as Self-Agent*

One dominant notion of person in narratives is person as agent. A narrative recounts the actions of its characters as one way of conveying the identities of these characters. In this, a narrative assumes that persons are agents, indeed self-agents, individuals capable of making decisions and acting on them. In light of narratives' reliance on person as self-agent, we can pursue our reflection on the identity of Jesus Christ by adopting the language of personal agency. That is, we can view Jesus Christ as a self-agent. This can be done in two steps. First, let us conceive of Jesus as a self-agent, similar to other women and men. Our historical narrative about Jesus will serve as the source for this. Second, let us consider Jesus Christ as God's agent, and, for this, we will turn again to Mark's Gospel.

Our understanding of Jesus as an ordinary self-agent can be developed from three angles. First, personal existence entails initiating a course of action and assuming responsibility for it. Taking responsibility for one's involvements presumes that one possesses the ability to reflect upon his or her engagements. In his discussion of personal agency Charles Taylor observes that "persons are a sub-class of agents."[32] They bring things about. What distinguishes persons however from other kinds of agents, for example, from machines and animals, is that "things matter to [persons]." They ask about the significance of their activities. So, for example, self-agents view their involvements in relation to moral standards.

An historical narrative of the sort with which we began this chapter presents Jesus as a self-agent. He brought things about within a vision and set of convictions. He displayed the ability to shape things as he saw fit. For instance, Jesus dined with a wide range of people—his disciples, tax collectors, Pharisees and the ritually impure. This was not happenstance. He chose to eat with groups of diverse people. Moreover, he told parables, stories about the seed, the vineyard tenants and the prodigal son, among others. He told stories not merely because he was an engaging storyteller, but because he had insight to convey. This behavior characterizes Jesus. He associated with diverse people, and he told stories that offered a fresh knowledge of God and the world.

Second, a person's intentions are exhibited in action. In this regard, G.E.M. Anscombe states: "Well, if you want to say at least some true things about a man's intentions, you will have a strong chance of success if you mention what he actually did or is doing.''[33] Anscombe uses the example of someone writing a letter. What does the person intend? To write to someone. Intentions are realized in actions. They are enacted. Therefore, we do not need to infer what someone had in mind when she did something. We need only describe what she did and the setting in which she did it, and we will comprehend what the person intended to do.

This logic is operative in an historical narrative about Jesus. Jesus' aims are evident in his actions. He dined with an odd assortment of people because he wanted to draw them into a new fellowship, founded on their relationship with him and the God he called Abba. What in fact occurred shows what Jesus intended: he wanted people to have a foretaste of the kingdom he proclaimed. So too his storytelling exhibits his intention. His parables disclose his understanding God's gracious care for creation, and Jesus intended his followers to do as God does. Jesus' intentions are not hidden behind his actions. Rather, they are realized in his table companionship and parables. Someone may want to say that Jesus was wrong in what he sought to show about God and human solidarity. What allows this disagreement is that we can grasp Jesus' intention in his actions.

Third, a person's words and deeds not only express what the person wants, but also disclose the person, the self. Gilbert Ryle has persuasively overturned "Descartes' myth" that the self is "a ghost in a machine."[34] There do not exist "two collateral histories," one of my physical activity and one of my inner self. No, a person unites both doing and thinking. Cornelius van Peursen expresses this view, when he states that "the 'I' of another person is manifested in all that he does. It is not something behind or among these doings of his, but is their total cohesion—is precisely that."[35] Therefore, what a person does reveals who she or he is.

An historical narrative can convey one sense of Jesus' identity. Jesus was a religious teacher who was viewed by some of his contemporaries as a troublemaker since he stirred up the people. He communicated his message in such an everyday activity as dining with others. He also taught through parables that even today engage us and question our outlooks on life. Further, this message was so important to him that he made personal sacrifices for it; for example, he suffered the misunderstanding of his relatives and townsfolk. He identified with his message to the extent that to reject his teaching was to spurn him. Indeed, this Jesus bound himself so completely to his message that he allowed himself to be put to death rather than to abandon his teaching—indeed, he envisioned his death as part of his message.

We do not know all we would like to know about Jesus' life and times, and we cannot depict in detail all Jesus said and did. Yet, this brief account suffices, for it provides a frame of reference in which to focus further on the identity of Jesus Christ. Jesus was a self-agent comparable to all men and women. This talk about Jesus as a self-agent equips us to delve more deeply into the image of Jesus Christ as founder, or, in Mark's terms, as the inaugurator of the kingdom.

III.2 *Jesus Christ, God's Agent*

While Jesus is a self-agent, as other men and women are self-agents, he is also a special case. As portrayed in the Gospels, he acts in ways that indicate his singular agency. For instance, he does not cower before death, but sees it as part of his mission. Moreover, he is not ultimately conquered by death, but realizes his intention to live in union with God. What does this say about him? How can we understand him better? We can see more deeply into his identity when we use the notions of person as self-agent and person as relation to reflect, first, on the bond between God and humankind, and, second, on Jesus Christ in Mark's Gospel.

The relationship between God and humankind is one of both unity and difference. Insofar as we are united with God, we receive the strength to be differentiated from God, to stand as human individuals in relation to God. Kasper puts it this way: "The greater the union with God, the greater the intrinsic reality of man."[36] In this view, God does not subsume humankind so that it loses its distinctiveness. On the contrary, God's Spirit draws women and men into the divine life so that they may participate as "the other" in union with God.

While this bond between God and humankind may at first appear odd, it makes greater sense when we consider human relationships in general. For instance, children gain the self-confidence to leave home as a result of the acceptance that marks their ties with parents and siblings.

Children who are affirmed and guided in their early years can mature to greater self-reliance that manifests itself as they form homes of their own. In contrast, abused or neglected children often have difficulty leaving home, either in a literal sense or figuratively. They may move out of their parents' house, but they may require years of therapy before they are no longer emotionally struggling with their families and gain a sense of independence. In a word, trust frees us, and distrust enslaves us. Our relating to God is no different. As we deepen our union with God, we are simultaneously enabled by God's Spirit to develop into individuals and a people distinct from the wellspring which nourishes us.

This general view applies to the case of Jesus Christ. He is the individual who has lived in total union with God, and therefore he is at the same time "the other," the "beloved." As Kasper writes: "[F]or love is, in an almost paradoxical way, the unity of two who, while remaining distinct and essentially free, nevertheless cannot exist the one without the other."[37] Jesus Christ is therefore the individual who is totally united with God and simultaneously possesses an identity of his own.

This account of the relationship between God and Jesus Christ sheds light on Jesus' identity, for it calls attention to his intimacy with God. Yet, this reflection can be taken even further. When we apply the notion of person as self-agent to Scripture, we can speak about Jesus Christ in even more specific terms. Previously, we viewed the historical figure of Jesus in relation to his actions, intentions and persistent self, and now we can use these same categories in relation to the protagonist of Mark's Gospel. In this, I shall draw on Hans Frei's *The Identity of Jesus Christ*.

Jesus' action in the course of Mark's Gospel reveals a shift *from power to powerlessness.*[38] At the outset, Jesus abruptly fills the gap formed by the arrest of John the Baptizer (Mk 1:14). He takes up the message that the kingdom is at hand. He calls Simon, James and John. He teaches in Capernaum's synagogue and exorcises a man "with an unclean spirit" (Mk 1:23) and then heals Simon Peter's mother-in-law. In the early part of his ministry Jesus is clearly in command of his activities throughout Galilee and beyond. After he returns to Galilee from Tyre and Sidon, however, things change.

As Jesus and his disciples journey to Caesarea Philippi, Peter identifies Jesus as "the Christ" (Mk 8:29). With this, Jesus declares that "the Son of man must suffer many things." From this point on, Jesus allows his adversaries to limit his activities. He performs fewer miracles.

He spends less time with "the multitude" and more with the disciples, instructing them so that they can carry on his mission without him. Jesus turns to Jerusalem (Mk 10:32), and the forces of Satan close in on him. His activity is confined to Jerusalem and Bethany. He is "seized" (Mk 14:46), and his movement is now dictated by others. He is "led" by guards to the court of the high priest. He is "led" to the palace of Pontius Pilate. He is "led" into the praetorium and scourged. Finally, he is "led" to Golgotha where he cries out "My God, my God, why hast thou forsaken me?" (Mk 15:34), and he dies. The protagonist who initially took charge of every situation takes his last breath nailed to a cross.

Jesus' conduct throughout this drama reveals his persistent intention. He has pledged *obedience to God*.[39] After his baptism, he is driven by the Spirit into the wilderness. He endures Satan's temptations and returns to Galilee to succeed John the Baptizer. After his initial appearances in Capernaum's synagogue and the house of Simon and Andrew, he withdraws to pray. When his "mother and brothers" are standing "outside," he explains: "Whoever does the will of God is my brother, and sister, and mother" (Mk 3:35). This dedication to God runs throughout the story, and it culminates in the garden of Gethsemane, when three times Jesus prays: "Abba, Father, all things are possible to thee; remove this cup from me; yet not what I will, but what thou wilt" (Mk 14:36).

Jesus has chosen to obey God, and he does this even to the point of being arrested, whipped and crucified. In other words, Jesus remains steadfast in his resolve to do God's will, and, as a result, he does not use force against his opponents, but allows them seemingly to control him. What is God's will? What is God's intention to which Jesus aligns his intention? In answering this question we discover the *unity and differentiation* between God and Jesus.[40]

Jesus declares God's will as he begins his ministry in Jerusalem: "For the Son of man also came not to be served but to serve, and to give his life as a ransom for many" (Mk 10:45). This is reiterated when in the upper room Jesus literally serves the disciples at table and, passing them the cup, announces: "This is my blood of the covenant, which is poured out for many" (Mk 14:24).

God's will therefore is that Jesus become weak, according to the world's standards. The change in Jesus' conduct, that is, from power to powerlessness, comes about because Jesus does not change his intention.

He seeks one thing: to do God's will. God's will for Jesus is dark, and yet it comes to light at the end of the drama.

When Jesus does not lash out at those who abuse him, his identity stands out. On the cross, he cries out and dies. The centurion observes this and says, "Truly this man was the Son of God!" (Mk 15:39). At the point where Jesus is wholly empty and must be filled by God, Jesus is most himself. Bound in obedience to God, Jesus relinquishes power, and when he is dead to self, he is fully alive in God. Then he is his true self, "the Son of God." This is confirmed when Mary Magdalene and Mary, the mother of James, and Salome visit the tomb. They are greeted by "a young man" who announces, "He has risen. . . . He is going before you to Galilee" (Mk 16:6-7).

Mark's Gospel displays what talk about unity and difference states. Jesus Christ so completely aligned his intention with God's intention that he is one with God and yet differentiated from God. He is God's agent, for he lived in complete obedience to God. Conforming his will to God's will meant living by God's rule (Mk 8:33), not by the human convention of countering violence with violence. At the very point of emptiness, Jesus was filled by God. Ironically, Jesus' surrender to Satan's twisted ways did not result in the loss of personal existence but in the manifestation of Jesus' authentic self: "Truly this man was the Son of God."

How then is this one life related to that of the human community? The answer, in short, is this: That to which all people aspire has already come about in Jesus Christ. All human agency occurs in varying degrees in union with God's agency. This Jesus has fully collaborated with God, and therefore he has assured the possibility of God's Spirit drawing all men and women into union with God, in relation to whom they receive their very selves. To return to our earlier images, Jesus Christ is the inaugurator of God's kingdom on earth. He is the founder of the new people who intend what God intends: to unite, through the Spirit, all of creation in God.[41]

This representation of Jesus Christ as God's agent is many-sided. It affords a fuller understanding of this person by highlighting his relationship to God. Further, it offers a way to grasp his "saving work." In this view, Jesus Christ has reconciled the human community with God, so that now all men and women, united with Jesus Christ, can collaborate with God's Spirit in bringing about the new creation. If space allowed these ideas could be developed further, especially by linking them with such Church teachings as Chalcedon's decree that Jesus Christ is "truly God" and "truly man." It suffices for now that we have seen how the use of narratives can enhance our attempts to identify Jesus Christ.

IV. *Narratives in a Christology of Reciprocity*

Our study of *Jesus the Christ,* in Chapter Two, has shown that Kasper's work provides a rich, identifying account of the one whom Christians call "Lord." According to Kasper, Jesus Christ is the mediator between God and creation. Yet, the exercise that we have undertaken demonstrates how a Christology of reciprocity can offer an even fuller identification of the Christ. This is possible by retelling the narratives that undergird the systematic inquiry. What I have done here is therefore to enlarge specific elements inherent in *Jesus the Christ.*

A Christology of reciprocity, says Kasper, depends on Scripture and tradition, historical study, and today's Church. In our inquiry these sources have been represented by three kinds of narrative: Gospel as story, an historical narrative, and biography. This emphasis upon narratives is not alien to *Jesus the Christ.* In speaking of historical research in Christology, Kasper states: "It has to narrate a real and actual story—history—and to bear testimony to it."[42] I have done this in recounting an historical narrative of Jesus. Moreover, narratives implicitly shape Kasper's discussion of tradition. The story of Philippians 2:6–11, for example, shapes his reflection on Jesus Christ as the Son of God. This is comparable to my use of Mark's Gospel.

This chapter's exercise has been guided not only by Kasper's work, but also by that of Schillebeeckx and van Beeck. Similar to *Jesus,* this inquiry has relied on an historical narrative about the Nazarean, and, similar to *Christ Proclaimed*, it has regarded the Gospels as stories. It has gone beyond Kasper, Schillebeeckx and van Beeck, however, in the use of Christian biography. There are precedents too for this usage. James McClendon, Jr., Brian McDermott, Leonardo Boff, and Terrence Tilley have already demonstrated how the witness of exemplary Christians can provide a rich source for theology.[43] In this chapter a biographical sketch of Dorothy Day has served as one expression of the contemporary Church's encounter with the living Christ.

In conclusion, one major difference between *Jesus the Christ* and the exercise of this chapter concerns the retelling of narratives within systematic inquiry. While Kasper leaves this form of discourse implicit within his "conscientious elucidation" of the confession that Jesus is the Christ, I have made it explicit in an exercise patterned after Kasper's Christology of reciprocity. The use of narratives in this chapter reflects the conviction expressed well by David Kelsey: "[Jesus] is known quite directly in and with the story, and recedes from cognitive grasp the more he is abstracted from the story."[44] This conviction needs to be discussed at greater length, and this is the task of the last chapter.[45]

NOTES

1. John Paul II, *Redeemer of Man* (Washington, D.C.: United States Catholic Conference, 1983), #21, p. 90.

2. Avery Dulles, *A Church To Believe In* (New York: Crossroad, 1982), pp. 1–18.

3. Dorothy Day's life is a source for Christology because she represents a vital movement today among Christians. Other women engaged in similar forms of outreach include Rosemary Haughton, Catherine de Hueck Doherty, Mother Teresa of Calcutta, and Sister Emmanuel in Cairo. On the norms for selecting biography in theology, see: Terrence W. Tilley, *Story Theology* (Wilmington: Michael Glazier, 1985), pp. 152–161; William A. Clebsch, *Christianity in European History* (New York: Oxford University Press, 1979), pp. 8–12; James Wm. McClendon, Jr., *Biography in Theology* (New York: Abingdon Press, 1974), pp. 39–40.

4. Cf. Frank Matera, *Passion Narratives and Gospel Theologies* (New York: Paulist Press, 1986); Donald Senior, *The Passion in Mark's Gospel* (New York: Paulist Press, 1985); David Rhoads and Donald Michie, *Mark as Story* (Philadelphia: Fortress Press, 1982); Norman Perrin and Dennis C. Duling, *The New Testament,* second edition (San Diego: Harcourt Brace Jovanovich, 1982), pp. 233–262; Sean Kealy, *Mark's Gospel: A History of Its Interpretation from the Beginnings Until 1979* (New York: Paulist Press, 1982); Werner Kelber, *Mark's Story of Jesus* (Philadelphia: Fortress Press, 1979); Robert Tannenhill, "The Gospel of Mark as Narrative Christology," *Semeia,* XVI (1979), 57–95; Paul Achtemeier, *Mark* (Philadelphia: Fortress Press, 1975).

5. Cf. Senior, *The Passion in Mark's Gospel,* pp. 150, 158.

6. On Mark's view of Jesus' resurrection, see: Rhoads and Michie, *Mark as Story,* p. 75.

7. Cf. John P. Meier, "Jesus Among the Historians," *The New York Times Book Review* (December 21, 1986), pp. 1, 16–19; Ernst P. Sanders, *Jesus and Judaism* (Philadelphia: Fortress Press, 1985); Jacob Neusner, *Judaism in the Beginning of Christianity* (Philadelphia: Fortress, 1984); Gerard Sloyan, *Jesus in Focus* (Mystic: Twenty-Third Publications, 1983); Joseph Fitzmyer, *A Christological Catechism,* (New York: Paulist, 1982); Anthony Harvey, *Jesus and the Constraints of History* (Philadelphia: Westminster, 1982); Josef Blank, *Der Jesus des Evangeliums* (Munich: Kosel, 1981); Günther Bornkamm, "Jesus Christ," in: *The Encyclopaedia Britannica,* fifteenth edition, Vol. X (1974), pp. 145–155.

8. Sean Freyne, *Galilee from Alexander the Great to Hadrian* (Wilmington and Notre Dame: Michael Glazier Press and University of Notre Dame Press, 1980), pp. 22–56, 138–54.

9. Geza Vermes, *Jesus and the World of Judaism* (Philadelphia: Fortress, 1984); *idem, Jesus the Jew* (Philadelphia: Fortress, 1981).

10. Norman Perrin, *Jesus and the Language of the Kingdom* (Philadelphia: Fortress, 1976); *idem, Rediscovering the Teaching of Jesus* (New York: Harper and Row), 1976.

11. Vermes, *Jesus and the World of Judaism,* pp. 39–43; James D. G. Dunn, *Christology in the Making* (Philadelphia: Westminster, 1980), pp. 12–33; Joseph Heinemann, *Prayer in the Talmud* (New York: Walter de Gruyter, 1977), 189–192; Martin Hengel, *The Son of God,* trans. John Bowden (Philadelphia: Fortress, 1976).

12. Cf. Reginald Fuller, *The Foundations of New Testament Christology* (New York: Charles Scribner's, 1965), pp. 46–61; Oscar Cullmann, *Christology of the New Testament,* trans. S. C. Guthrie and C. Hall (Philadelphia: Westminster, 1959), pp. 13–50; Richard N. Longenecker, *The Christology of Early Jewish Christianity* (Naperville: Alec R. Allenson, 1970), pp. 32–39.

13. Dorothy Day, *The Long Loneliness* (New York: Curtis Books, 1952), p. 9. Cf. Jim Forest, *Love Is the Measure* (New York: Paulist Press, 1986); William Miller, *Dorothy Day* (San Francisco: Harper and Row, 1982).

14. On the Catholic Worker movement, see: Mel Piehl, *Breaking Bread* (Philadelphia: Temple University Press, 1983).

15. On conversion, see: Walter Conn, *Christian Conversion* (New York: Paulist Press, 1986).

16. Day, *The Long Loneliness,* p. 231.

17. Cf. Monika Hellwig, *The Compassion of God* (Wilmington: Michael Glazier, 1984); Henri Nouwen, Donald McNeill and Douglas Morrison, *Compassion* (Garden City: Doubleday, 1982).

18. Cf. Gerhard Von Rad, *Old Testament Theology,* I, trans. D. M. G. Stalker (New York: Harper and Row, 1962), pp. 139–153, 179–186.

19. Cf. Eduard Löhse, *Colossians and Philemon*, trans. W. R. Poehlmann and R. J. Karris (Philadelphia: Fortress Press, 1971), pp. 41–61.

20. On Jesus and the founding of the Church, see: Francis Schüssler Fiorenza, *Foundational Theology* (New York: Crossroad, 1984), pp. 59–192.

21. Cf. Gerhard Lohfink, *Jesus and Community*, trans. by John P. Galvin (New York: Paulist, 1984).

22. Cf. Rhoades and Michie, *Mark as Story*, *passim*.

23. Dorothy Day, *Meditations*, selected and arranged by Stanley Vishnewski (New York: Paulist, 1970), p. 34.

24. Cf. Carroll Stuhlmueller, "The Foundations for Mission in the Old Testament," in: Donald Senior and C. Stuhlmueller (eds.), *The Biblical Foundations for Mission* (Maryknoll: Orbis, 1983), pp. 9–140.

25. Cf. Donald Senior, "The Foundations for Mission in the New Testament," in: *idem, The Biblical Foundations for Mission*, pp. 141–160.

26. *Ibid.*, pp. 211–232; Senior, *The Passion of Jesus in the Gospel of Mark*, *passim*.

27. Day, *Meditations*, p. 68.

28. Cf. John L. McKenzie, "Aspects of Old Testament Thought," in: Raymond Brown *et al.* (eds.), *The Jerome Biblical Commentary*, II (Englewood Cliffs: Prentice-Hall, 1968), pp. 752–753; cf. Nelson Glueck, *"Hesed" in the Bible*, trans. by A. Gottschalk (Cincinnati: The Hebrew Union College Press, 1967).

29. Cf. Hellwig, *Jesus, the Compassion of God;* Gerald O'Collins, *The Calvary Christ* (Philadelphia: Westminster, 1977).

30. Senior, *The Passion of Jesus in the Gospel of Mark*, pp. 139–147; cf. John C. Dwyer, *Son of Man, Son of God* (New York: Paulist, 1983).

31. Day, *Meditations*, p. 64.

32. Charles Taylor, *Human Agency and Language* (Cambridge: Cambridge University Press, 1985), p. 97.

33. Gertrude E. M. Anscombe, *Intention*, second edition (Ithaca: Cornell University Press, 1963), p. 8. Cf. Stuart Hampshire, *Thought and Action*, new edition (Notre Dame: University of Notre Dame Press, 1982), pp. 90–168.

34. Gilbert Ryle, *The Concept of Mind* (New York: Barnes and Noble Books, 1949), p. 15.

35. Cornelius van Peursen, *Body, Soul, Spirit* (London: Oxford University Press, 1966), p. 153.

36. Walter Kasper, *Jesus the Christ*, trans. V. Green (New York: Paulist Press, 1976), p. 248.

37. *Ibid.*, p. 249.

38. Hans W. Frei, *The Identity of Jesus Christ* (Philadelphia: Fortress Press, 1975), pp. 102–115.

39. *Ibid.*, pp. 108–111.

40. *Ibid.*, pp. 116–125.

41. This representation of Jesus Christ is similar to: Kasper, *Jesus the Christ*, p. 100; Wolfhart Pannenberg, *Jesus—God and Man*, trans. L. L. Wilkins and D. A. Priebe (Philadelphia: The Westminster Press, 1968), pp. 365–378; Karl Barth, *Church Dogmatics*, II/2, ed. G. W. Bromiley (Edinburgh: T. & T. Clark, 1957), p. 177; cf. *idem, Church Dogmatics*, IV/2, ed. G. W. Bromiley (Edinburgh: T. & T. Clark, 1958), p. 764.

42. Kasper, *Jesus the Christ*, p. 20.

43. Tilley, *Story Theology*, pp. 147–181; Brian McDermott, "The Christ Wound," *Word and Spirit*, IV (1983), pp. 32–53; Leonardo Boff, *St. Francis: A Model for Human Liberation* (New York: Crossroad, 1982); McClendon, *Biography as Theology*.

44. David Kelsey, *The Uses of Scripture in Recent Theology* (Philadelphia: Fortress Press, 1975), p. 39.

45. My conviction has been shaped by John Shea, *The Challenge of Jesus* (Garden City: Doubleday, 1977) and John Dunne, *A Search for God in Time and Memory* (New York: Macmillan, 1967).

Chapter Six

NARRATIVES IN CHRISTOLOGY

An urgent question for Christians today is found at the heart of Mark's Gospel: "And [Jesus] asked them, 'But who do you say that I am?' " (Mk 8:27). To some extent, of course, this question confronts Christians in every age. As William Clebsch writes: "The history of Christianity is haunted in every period with concern for understanding the personhood and personal identity of the religion's savior."[1] But it is also true that this question strikes contemporary Christians with a special force. To confirm this one need only note the spate of Christological texts over the past two decades. We have an insatiable appetite for Jesus-talk.

An investigation into Jesus' identity can employ narratives, and it can do this in more than one way. In *Jesus* Edward Schillebeeckx has portrayed Jesus of Nazareth by fashioning an historical narrative about him. Further, Frans Jozef van Beeck has discussed the risen Christ in *Christ Proclaimed* by recounting the narrative that runs through the Gospels of Matthew, Mark and Luke. Yet, these distinct kinds of narrative can also be integrated by using a single, systematic endeavor of the sort exhibited by Walter Kasper in *Jesus the Christ*. The sources for Christology—Scripture and tradition, history and today's Church—provide us with biblical stories, historical narratives and Christian biographies that produce complementary images of Jesus Christ, and we can employ these images in our answer to the question: "Who is Jesus Christ today?"

These different ways of using narratives in Christology share the conviction that narratives enable us to know aspects of reality that we would otherwise miss. We recount a series of events and what people said and did, because these recollections are in fact forms of knowing events and people. We tell stories about God because they permit us to gain some sense of God's interventions in human affairs.[2] Thus, narratives are included in theology to do more than to embellish an idea that is already clear. They function in our reflections on God, Jesus Christ, and God's encounters with us so that we can understand, at least to some degree, the divine reality, the character of God. As Johann Baptist Metz states: "Stories of conversion and memories of exodus are therefore not simply dramatic embellishments of a previously conceived 'pure' theology. On the contrary they form part of the basic structure of this theology."[3]

This conviction, operative in the past five chapters, can now be explored in three claims. First, personal existence is like a narrative. In *After Virtue* Alasdair MacIntyre has argued that we can know who we are when we envisage our lives as histories with a beginning, a middle and an end.[4] This view can be extended to Jesus Christ, for his "life" too can be seen as a narrative, though one that breaks our customary sense of time and space.

Second, both historical narratives and fictional narratives can contribute simultaneously to our knowledge of a person. In his essay "The Narrative Function" Paul Ricoeur has demonstrated that history and fiction possess a common structure and a common referent.[5] As a result, while they are indeed separate kinds of narratives, they can shed light on the same life. This insight can be employed not only in our knowledge of other persons in general, but also in Christology. Historical narratives, the Gospels, and biographies of exemplary Christians are very different kinds of narratives, and yet they can deepen our understanding of the same individual, Jesus Christ.

Third, a theologian's explicit use of narratives need not reduce Christology to storytelling, but can give specificity to the notions of person at work in a systematic inquiry. Both Schillebeeckx and Ricoeur have maintained that narratives can generate the images and models which undergird conceptual discourse. In support of this view we need only recall what we have seen in van Beeck's *Christ Proclaimed,* in our Christological exercise (Chapter Five), and in Kasper's *Jesus the Christ.*

My discussion of these three claims—regarding personal life as a narrative, the use of diverse kinds of narratives, and the linkage between narrative and conceptual discourse—has a modest goal. It is meant to clarify the logic of using narratives in Christology. I do not intend to provide a theory about narratives, nor do I wish to give a justification or *apologia* for narratives in theology. This chapter simply describes how our reliance on narratives in ordinary discourse can be intelligibly extended to systematic theology.[6]

I.1 *A Person's Life as a Narrative*

We often rely on biography when we want to identify someone. This observation was made in Chapter One, but no explanation was given. Now I wish to show why this is so, by considering the narrative character of personal existence. In recent years, arguments for this view of human life as a narrative have been made on the basis of the temporality of personal experience (e.g., by Stephen Crites), aesthetics and experience (e.g., by Barbara Hardy), and the intelligibility of human action (e.g., by Alasdair MacIntyre).[7] This last kind of argument is adopted here, since it aligns with the previous chapter's discussion of Jesus Christ as self-agent, as one known in his actions.

In *After Virtue* Alasdair MacIntyre maintains that a proper comprehension of the virtues depends upon the idea that personal existence possesses a coherence, a unity in which each part fits within the whole. The commitment to truth, justice and beauty is not confined to one sector of a person's involvements (for example, to dealings with one's professional associates). Rather this commitment naturally tends to pervade all areas of life, one's whole self. How then are we to conceive of this self which is the subject of this commitment along with others? We should hold ''a concept of a self,'' MacIntyre argues, ''whose unity resides in the unity of a narrative which links birth to life to death as narrative beginning to middle to end.''[8] Such a view, he notes, goes against our modern tendency to break up reality (and hence our lives) into small segments. We can see the value of this concept of person when we consider that our understanding of human behavior rests on our grasp of three dimensions to that behavior which can be identified as its history, its intention and its narrative form.

Imagine, says MacIntyre, that we see our neighbor digging in his backyard. We make sense of this activity by situating it within various settings. One of these might be the man's history. Many years ago when he married, he learned of his wife's delight in a vegetable garden, and so every spring he turns the earth and plants onions, tomatoes and beans out of love for her. Yet, this is not the only possible setting for this action. Another might be the history of the property. Long before the husband and wife bought the house, it had a vegetable garden. The man's digging therefore also makes sense in that he is upholding the plot's heritage. As this example shows, one thing we do to grasp the sense of a person's action is to place it in its historical context.

Another thing we try to do is to find out what the person has in mind, what the person is hoping to achieve in doing something. To return to our example, the neighbor could tell us that he is doing it for the physical exercise, that he is planting for a mid-summer crop, that he is pleasing his wife, or that he is keeping up the custom on this land. As these hypothetical answers suggest, there may be more than one intention involved in undertaking any given activity, and these intentions might not all be realized at the same time. The neighbor's immediate aim may be to get exercise; a long range goal may be to please his wife; an even longer range intention may be to sustain the land's heritage. Therefore, a second way in which we understand a person's behavior is in relation to his or her short-term and long-term intentions.

Once we recognize the importance of history and intentionality for a proper understanding of a person's action, we can easily grasp the role of narrative here as well. If we know a person's action, its settings and its intentions, we have in hand the stuff of drama. Our task then is to figure out how these elements are ordered in the person's life. In other words, when we seek to understand someone's behavior, we are trying to detect the narrative that the person in fact lives. MacIntyre writes: "Narrative history of a certain kind turns out to be the basic and essential genre for the characterization of human actions."[9]

Our lives are best seen, contends MacIntyre, as "enacted narratives."[10] We in fact live out dramas with beginnings, middles and ends, and at some point during or after these connected events we are sometimes able to recount the narrative we were living out. First come the narratives, the histories, in which we participate, and then in retrospect we recount these events in the narratives we tell about our lives. In MacIntyre's words: "Stories are lived before they are told—except in the case of fiction."

Personal existence possesses two qualities that are also found in narratives. Our lives are goal-oriented and yet remain unpredictable. We rarely find ourselves realizing our intentions precisely as we had originally conceived them, for accidents and other people's interests make us change our plans. Yet, we continue to plan and envision a goal (a *telos*) or goals for ourselves. We anticipate a future, even while we cannot predict it. These features of purposefulness and contingency are also inherent in narratives. Narratives spring from the conflict between what characters set out to do and what in fact happens to them, and this is the very tension that marks our lives.

Finally, these reflections on how we understand a person's conduct lead to a fresh concept of personal identity. The conventional idea since the Enlightenment is derived from John Locke (d. 1704) and David Hume (d. 1776) who, notes MacIntyre, viewed personal existence "atomistically." That is, they maintained that personal identity could not be linked with a person's physical qualities nor to one's history, since these change. It had to consist of some "inner," permanent element that could be isolated from the other empirical parts of human life. This reductionistic view narrows down the continuity in a person's life to something mental, and it has resulted in contemporary analytical philosophers speaking of personal identity in terms of "psychological states or events."

This approach is flawed, argues MacIntyre, for it defines a "self," and hence "personal identity," independently of the history and intentions of that self. It ignores the very contexts which allow us to know not only a person's intentions and actions, but also the person herself. Just as a person's actions have to be understood within their respective histories, so too the person's identity can only be adequately comprehended in relation to his or her direction in life, his or her background. "That background," insists MacIntyre, "is provided by the concept of a story and of that kind of unity of character which a story requires."[11] A person's identity is therefore discovered in an actual or enacted narrative that the person has lived out. Once this narrative is known, for example in a biography, then this account can yield an idea of person. Or, as MacIntyre states: "[T]he concept of a person is that of a character abstracted from a history."

This "narrative concept of selfhood," observes MacIntyre, makes two demands upon us. First, it highlights that I am accountable for what I have done. It assumes that I am a continuous self, the persistent character in a narrative. In MacIntyre's words: "I am what I may justifiably be taken by others to be in the course of living out a story that runs from my birth to my death.'' As a consequence, I am responsible for what I have engaged in at any point in this history, even though that action may be long past.

Second, not only am I responsible for my involvements, but I can ask other persons to be responsible for theirs. I can do so, because the narrative understanding of personal identity assumes that we are part of one another's histories. "The narrative of any one life is," says Mac-Intyre, "part of an interlocking set of narratives."[12] Our lives, our narratives, are intertwined, and therefore you can require that I give an account of my behavior, and I can demand the same of you.

MacIntyre embarked on this inquiry about how we know another person in order to establish a concept of self adequate to a discussion of the virtues. This concept is that the self, and hence personal identity, is "the unity of a narrative embodied in a single life." In light of this, MacIntyre argues that the virtues are not traits belonging to only one aspect of our lives. Rather they are qualities manifest in our whole selves, in the narratives that we live. Persons of virtue enact narratives that display truth and justice and beauty.

Further, MacIntyre's account provides an answer to our immediate question. Why do we look for a biography when we want to know who someone is? Why do we recall someone's words and deeds when we want to explain who he or she is? We do so because a person's life is a unity comparable to that of a narrative. In other words, MacIntyre's understanding of personal existence corroborates the notion of personal identity laid out in the first chapter. There I proposed that a person's identity consists of the length, breadth and depth of his or her life. That is, the "I" is the result of the person's history, bonds with others, and self-understanding, and we now see that these elements are woven together in a narrative, especially in a biography.

I.2 *The Narrative Character of Jesus Christ*

The view of a person's life as an enacted narrative sheds light on personal existence in general, and it also clarifies Christian convictions concerning the reality of Jesus Christ. According to Christian belief, Christ's "life" manifests a unity—a unity that extends even beyond death. The person who was baptized by John in the Jordan River is the same person who, after his crucifixion, appeared to the disciples. For Christians, therefore, this life possesses a unity beyond death—a unity that can be envisaged as a narrative. To quote Metz: "The logos of the cross and resurrection has a narrative structure."[13] The significance of this view of Christ becomes clearer if we consider the settings in which Christians locate Jesus' words and deeds.

Human conduct becomes intelligible, observes MacIntyre, when it is set within its appropriate contexts, and this applies to Jesus Christ. Noteworthy actions in Jesus' life include his use of Abba, his parables on God's kingdom and his table companionship. Significant events in his life would obviously include his birth and his crucifixion. The meaning of these occurrences comes to light as they are placed within their settings. What are these contexts?

One setting for the actions and events in Jesus' life is an historical narrative of the sort fashioned by Schillebeeckx in *Jesus* and also presented in the previous chapter. In this kind of setting, Jesus' use of Abba manifests his sense of intimacy with God, while his parables of the kingdom and table fellowship display his understanding of this God. Further, his birth and death constitute the beginning and end of what from one perspective is an ordinary human life. Yet his death on the cross adds a note of ambiguity to this life. Was he a true herald, indeed the latter-day prophet, or a false prophet? Was he a true religious teacher, or was he a blasphemer? How one answers these questions determines how one makes sense out of all of the actions and events in this life. But in any case, this historical narrative provides one setting for Jesus' words and deeds.

A second possible context is the view of Jesus' life as a narrative that fractures our sense of time. One such version of this, upon which Kasper relies in *Jesus the Christ,* is the kenosis hymn of Philippians 2:6–11:[14]

> . . . Christ Jesus, who, though he was in the form of God . . . emptied himself, taking the form of a servant, being born in the likeness of men. And . . . he humbled himself and became obedient unto death, even death on a cross. Therefore God highly exalted him and bestowed on him the name that is above every name . . . Jesus Christ is Lord, to the glory of God the Father.

In this setting Jesus' actions and the events of his life make sense in relation to his obedience. He addresses God as Abba because he is united with God, and he tells parables about the kingdom and dines in mixed company because he is fulfilling God's intention to reconcile all people with God. Further, Jesus' birth and death are not the beginning and end of an ordinary life, but the middle period of this "life." Jesus' earthly existence is one phase in the larger drama of his obedience to the God who is reaching out to humankind.[15] The cross therefore loses its ambiguity, and it appears as the culminating point in a life dedicated to God.

This reflection on the appropriate settings for Jesus' actions reminds us that for Christians the unity of his life goes beyond death. An historical narrative provides one context for Jesus' words and deeds, but it is not the primary one. The occurrences in this life must be situated within a larger context, namely a narrative that breaks our ordinary sense of time and space. In light of MacIntyre's discussion, we can pursue this narrative view of Jesus Christ even further.

A narrative is a recital of events. It is an account with a beginning, a middle and an end. In a strictly historical perspective, Jesus' life begins in approximately 4 B.C.E., it reaches its most public expression during Jesus' few years of ministry, and it ends in approximately 30 C.E. Here, then, is one view of Jesus Christ's enacted narrative. Yet, from the perspective of Christian faith, this account is too narrow. It needs to be embedded within a larger "history."

Talk of the beginning, middle and end of Christ's life puts the terms "beginning," "end," and "middle" to an odd use. This ending does not occur at death but beyond it. It is not an ending as much as a beginning, for it creates a future. This is conveyed in the first Christians' prayer: "Come, Lord Jesus" (Rev 22:20). Moreover, it is sustained by the Church throughout the centuries. For example, at the Eucharist Christians confess the memorial acclamation: "Christ has died, Christ is risen, Christ will come again." For this community, Christ's ending is in fact an open future.

This sense of Christ's life beyond death entails two dimensions. First, Christ continues to abide in history. This "realized eschatology" is implied in the Eucharist's memorial acclamation: "Christ is risen." It is made concrete, for instance, when Brother Roger Schutz of Taizé observes that Christ suffers with all who suffer and rejoices with all who are rejoicing.[16] The risen Christ continues to abide with us. Second, Christ will bring history as we know it to a close and institute God's new creation. This "futuristic eschatology" is conveyed in the memorial acclamation: "Christ will come again." The risen Christ will be fully manifest in the future.

Further, the view that Christ's ending initiates an open future influences how Christians understand the beginning and middle of Jesus' life. In John's Gospel, for example, this life starts prior to birth. According to John, this life originated "in the beginning" (Jn 1:1), and therefore its "beginning" is unlike the births and commencements with which we are familiar. Moreover, in this perspective, the "middle" of Christ's life consists of not simply his two or three years of public ministry, but his entire historical existence. Hence, a three-stage Christology appears, for instance, in John 1:14: "The Word was made flesh, and dwelt among us." At the outset the Logos exists with God, then he enters into human affairs, and finally he returns to God.

This perspective on Christ's life shows something striking. Even though the beginning, middle and ending of this existence fracture the conventional understanding of time and space, the unity of this life is still manifest in the form of a narrative. A series of "events" are recited in the ancient kerygma: "that Christ died . . . that he was buried, that he was raised . . . that he appeared to Cephas, then to the twelve" (1 Cor 15:3–5). A recital of "events" also occurs in the Eucharist's memorial acclamation: "Christ has died, Christ is risen, Christ will come again." Though Jesus' "story" disrupts our normal understanding of space and time, we still speak of his life as a narrative.

Let us sum up. In the Christian view, the unity of Jesus Christ's life is an actual narrative that begins before time, runs through history, and reaches into the future. This view of Christ emerges when Christians locate the actions and events of his life within their appropriate settings. An historical narrative only partially reveals the meaning of Jesus' actions. A larger narrative is required—a narrative of the sort implied in the Eucharist's memorial acclamation: "Christ has died, Christ is risen, Christ will come again." Stories about Jesus Christ, in particular the Gospels, do not therefore impose a narrative shape upon a non-narrative reality. Rather these stories express this life's inherent narrative. This recognition leads however to another issue: What is the logic of recounting different kinds of narratives about Jesus Christ?

II.1 *History and Fiction: Sense and Reference*

If personal existence in general and the life of Christ in particular possess a narrative character, then the issue arises as to how we can best understand a person, an enacted narrative. Should we rely only on one kind of narrative, for example on biography, for our knowledge of another person? Or would we attain a fuller knowledge of the person by complementing biography with another kind of narrative, for example, with fiction? I favor the use of different kinds of narratives, and I shall develop this view in a claim consisting of two parts. First, we can indeed strengthen our knowledge of others through the use of fiction as well as biography. Second, this logic extends to our knowledge of Jesus Christ. But instead of relying on biography and fiction, in this special case we can employ historical narrative, Gospel and Christian biography.

Paul Ricoeur has in fact already argued for the first point. In his essay "The Narrative Function" Ricoeur maintains that history and fiction complement each other in our inquiries into the human condition. Our human condition is marked by our "historicity," by our essential involvement in history, and this activity is expressed both in history and in fiction, each of which refers to an aspect of our historical being. Ricoeur's general point is "that the historicity of human experience can be brought to language only as narrativity, and moreover that this narrativity itself can be articulated only by the crossed interplay of the two narrative modes."[17] This idea is presented in two more specific theses: first, that history and fiction are forms of the category narrative, and, second, that history and fiction possess the same referent.

According to Ricoeur, the key to grasping "the structural unity of historical and fictional narratives" is plot. Plot, as defined by Robert Scholes and Robert Kellogg, is "the dynamic, sequential element in narrative literature."[18] This definition is developed further by Ricoeur who observes that plot in fact possesses two dimensions. On the one hand, it is sequential. It recites a series of episodes, and hence it has an "episodic dimension." On the other hand, this recollection orders these events, at least in some loose arrangement. By linking the episodes, plot possesses a "configurational dimension." Given its two dimensions, plot is therefore an intricate, "paradoxical" structure. This means, notes Ricoeur, "that the most humble narrative is always more than a chronological series of events, and, in turn, that the configurational dimension cannot eclipse the episodic dimension without abolishing the narrative structure itself.''[19] Plot's episodic and configurational structure has bearing upon our understanding of history and fiction.

History, contends Ricoeur, depends upon narrative and in particular upon plot. Historians derive their data from other people's accounts, for example, from chronicles, memoirs and reports. These materials are themselves narratives, or, when assembled, they are elements in a chronology. In turn, these recitals of events serve as the implicit or explicit context for historical explanations. Historians either recount a series of events or presuppose this series, and then, in relation to this, they explain why events occurred as they did.

What affords this transition from narrative to theoretical discourse? This shift comes about because of plot's configurational dimension. Plot yields the images and models from which the historian explains what occurred according to history's "laws." In fact, historical explanations function as aids for following the original narratives. They call attention to the forces at work in the drama. History is therefore a form of narrative.

Fiction too depends upon plot. It relies on both plot's configurational dimension and its episodic dimension. Fiction, insists Ricoeur, is constituted by its "irreducible temporality."[20] That is, fiction depends upon a movement from one state of affairs to another. It entails a quest, and this quest necessarily involves a series of episodes. As Ricoeur observes, "the whole movement from contract to conflict, from alienation to the restoration of order, is *successive by nature.*" This succession from one episode to another is sequential, and therefore it manifests fiction's essential reliance on plot. Fiction is a form of narrative.

The first conclusion is therefore that, despite their differences, history and fiction rely on a common structure. In Ricoeur's words: "The two separate analyses which we have just made of the role of plot in historical narrative and fictional narrative suggest the idea of a family resemblance at the level of sense or structure between these two narrative types."[21] This concretely means, for example, that Carl Sandburg's *Abraham Lincoln: The War Years* (1939) and Gore Vidal's *Lincoln* (1984) possess a structural unity. Though the former is history, more specifically biography, and the latter is fiction, both manifest the same form, namely narrative.

Recognition of this similarity between these distinct kinds of narrative leads then to the second question: Do history and fiction also share the same referent? This query's answer is Ricoeur's second thesis: History and fiction possess a "unity of reference." This thesis is elucidated in three "propositions."

First, history or, more accurately, historiography entails not only attentiveness to "real events in the real world" ("historio-"), it also requires writing ("-graphy"). Contrary to the positivist view, the historian's craft demands an act of imagination, what R. G. Collingwood called "imaginative reconstruction." Historians assemble their material from chronicles and reports, and this assembling involves configuring this material in such a way that it provides an "indirect reference" to reality. Thus, Hayden White has persuasively argued, notes Ricoeur, that a history is a "literary artifact." It is created through historians' figurative skills as well as their critical skills.

Second, fiction manifests our involvement in history by being mimetic, imitative, of our activities. This act of representing reality is not however simply a matter of superficial imitation. On the one hand, it is directed toward reality, thereby requiring a grasp of events' essence or "logical structure." On the other hand, it distances itself from everyday reality by means of a "productive imagination," an imagination that fashions unusual representations of the "real world." Fiction reveals the world's hidden dynamics in images that are seemingly unrelated to ordinary reality so that, by appearing unfamiliar, the familiar is perceived in depth. Therefore, by means of its "split or cleft reference," fiction in fact affords insight into our historicity. Ricoeur states: "This suspension of the relation to the world is only the negative counterpart of a more fundamental relation [to the world—a relation] which is precisely that of a productive reference."[22]

Third, history and fiction provide distinct kinds of insight into the same reality. According to Ricoeur, "the references of 'true history' and 'fictional history' *cross* upon the basic historicity of human experience." Both forms of narrative are intended to communicate something about our human condition. On the one hand, historians convey what we can learn from the past. By clarifying the values earlier peoples lived by and what these led to, historians call attention to what is possible today, to "the buried potentialities of the present." On the other hand, storytellers are not bound to the contingencies of what has actually occurred in human affairs. They are free to explore the depths of the human spirit, *"the heart of the real world of action.*''[23] Therefore, both kinds of narrative refer to our state as historical beings. History shows what is possible, and fiction reveals "what is essential in reality."

Ricoeur's three propositions can be expressed concretely by considering, as a case in point, the "cross references" of Sandburg's *Abraham Lincoln* and Vidal's *Lincoln*. On the one hand, as a literary artifact, the biography not only presents data about the sixteenth President of the United States, it also arranges this so that a specific image is projected. On the other hand, Vidal's *Lincoln* is mimetic. It produces a representation of the interaction between the sixteenth President and his situation—a representation that may not be factually accurate in each of its details, but may accurately portray motives, feelings and convictions. Finally, the references of *Abraham Lincoln* and of *Lincoln* "cross" in this way: the biography conveys both what was actually possible in Lincoln's life and also what is possible in the American presidency today in light of an earlier precedent, and the novel offers one perception of Lincoln's essence or character while also shedding light on the vision, ambitions and manipulation that can emerge in the leading of a nation.

In "The Narrative Function," Ricoeur takes a step toward a "general theory of narrative" by reflecting on the sense and reference of history and fiction. Convinced that human experience gains expression in "narrativity," he pursues the idea that "this narrativity itself can be articulated only by the crossed interplay of two narrative modes." His first thesis is therefore that history and fiction belong to the same category. They are forms of narrative. His second thesis is that while history yields an "indirect reference" to reality and fiction a "cleft reference," these genres do in fact treat two dimensions of the same reality.

These reflections on history and fiction are stimulating in general. They contribute to our recovery of a long neglected form of cognition—narrative.[24] Also, Ricoeur's thought is particularly helpful for reflecting on the roles of different kinds of narratives in our talk about God.[25] Before his views on fiction can be adopted in theology, however, one distinction needs to be recalled. In Chapter One, I proposed that the category story has two sub-categories, fiction and non-fiction. In "The Narrative Function" Ricoeur has discussed only fictional stories, but his views can be extended to non-fictional stories, namely, to the Gospels. This is what I will do in a reflection on the function of historical narratives and the Gospels in Christology.

II.2 *Historical Narratives and Gospel*

In the course of this book I have argued for the use of different kinds of narratives in Christology. This method is found in a Christology of reciprocity, as exhibited in Kasper's *Jesus the Christ,* for this approach brings together Scripture and tradition, historical research, and contemporary thought, and these sources implicitly include various forms of narrative. I have proposed that this approach can be enhanced through the explicit use of historical narratives about Jesus, of the Gospels as stories, and of biographies of exemplary Christians. While at first glance this confluence of narratives may appear odd, this method's logic is illumined by Ricoeur's comments on the complementarity of history and fiction. This can be shown by discussing the sense and reference of an historical narrative about Jesus and the Gospels, and afterward considering biography. Let us pursue then two questions. First, in what way do historical narrative and Gospel manifest the same structure? Second, in what ways are they referring to the same reality?

As Ricoeur has shown, history and fiction belong to the category "narrative." Can the same be said of historical narratives and the Gospels? According to William Poteat, story, which includes fiction though is not limited to it, is "a temporal deployment of events" requiring the concepts "person" and "action," and history is "a similar temporal deployment of events, bound to . . . 'facts'."[26] In contrast to both story and history, myth does not rely on notions of person and action, for its characters are archetypes and its movement is circular. Given these definitions, we cannot provide a history of Jesus; we simply lack the materials for his biography. Yet we can recount in a loose way the events in his life, and this recollection constitutes an historical narrative, or what Schillebeeckx calls a "post-critical narrative history."[27] Granted then that this is a form of narrative, how do we classify the accounts of Matthew, Mark, Luke and John?

Following Poteat's definition, we can say that each of the Gospels is a story. Each recounts a sequence of events dependent upon the concepts "person" and "action." A Gospel is a narrative, an account with a beginning, a middle, and an ending—a narrative in which specific agents act and suffer in lifelike circumstances. Hence, a Gospel is not a myth, but a story. But this is not to say that a Gospel is a fiction, if "fiction" is taken to mean an account having little or no regard for historical facts. A Gospel rests on a substratum of historical facts, and it unites historical data and images within a community's testimony to an historical person. A Gospel is not a fictional story, but a non-fictional story.[28] This recognition leads to our second question.

How do historical narratives and Gospels refer to Jesus? An historical narrative's reference is that of a history. In Ricoeur's terms, it is an indirect reference, for it relies on others' recollections and testimonies, especially as found in the Gospels. It aims at historical accuracy, presenting Jesus according to the criteria of modern historiography. The kind of reference afforded by the Gospels is however harder to place.

The Gospels' reference is similar to the cleft reference of fiction. The Gospels ask their hearers to suspend their judgment about what is possible and, in doing this, to follow the narrative on its own terms. The Gospels' reference cannot therefore be determined apart from their verbal sense. The Gospels are thus to a large extent self-referential. As Hans Frei states: "We cannot have what [the Gospels] are about (the 'subject matter') without the stories themselves. They are history-like precisely because like history-writing and the traditional novel and unlike myths and allegories they literally mean what they say."[29]

The Gospels' reference is not however solely identical with their sense. If it were, there would be no point in Christology's reliance on an historical narrative along with the Gospels. Here is where Ricoeur's thought is helpful. Using his categories, we can say that the person of whom the Gospels speak is indeed known in these stories, and yet he is simultaneously accessible in other ways. Various kinds of accounts are fashioned about this Jesus, and one type must not be measured against another, since each offers a distinct perspective on this person. While the Gospels are one form of testimony, historical narratives are another.

Recognition of an historical narrative's indirect reference and the Gospels' cleft reference puts us in a position to see some of what occurs when these two kinds of narratives are brought together in a Christology of reciprocity. According to Ricoeur the references of history and fiction "cross" upon our historicity. That is, each shows some dimension of our activities. In a parallel way, the references of historical narrative and Gospel cross upon the reality of Jesus Christ. These two types of accounts apprehend Jesus Christ from distinct points of view. This logic can be glimpsed in two steps.

First, historical narratives and the Gospels are complementary. On the one hand, historical narratives stem from historians' productive imagination.[30] They result from the historian's skills in configuring the data. On the other hand, the Gospels are mimetic: they are intended to represent the person whom the disciples knew both before and after his death. They are not meant to allow their readers escape from reality, for example, as some forms of fiction do. Rather they are directed at the tragedy and hope found in one actual life. The upshot is that historical narratives bear a basic resemblance to the Gospels, and conversely the Gospels hold a deep similarity to historical narratives.

Second, historical narratives and the Gospels pursue a similar goal. Both are told in order to communicate something about this Jesus. Historical narratives are recounted with a view to showing the possibilities facing Jesus and what he in fact chose to do, for example, that he could have fled Jerusalem, but instead allowed himself to be arrested. In highlighting Jesus' options, historical narratives also afford a glimpse of what Ricoeur calls our "potentialities," for instance, our readiness to suffer for our convictions. Further, the Gospels disclose the "essence" of this Jesus, for example, his filial intimacy with God and his unwavering dedication to his mission.

Ricoeur's categories clarify the use of two different kinds of narratives in Christology. Historical narratives and the Gospels possess a structural unity in that both are forms of narrative, and further the references of these two types of accounts converge on the person of Jesus Christ. This account sheds light on why both historical narratives and the Gospels have valid roles to play in a Christology of reciprocity. It shows that the uniting of historical research and tradition, as seen for instance in Kasper's *Jesus the Christ,* follows a rationale similar to that found in our reliance on both history and fiction. In light of this reflection, we can consider Christian biography in Christology.

II.3 *Biography in Christology*

"Christological knowledge," writes Metz, "is formed and handed on not primarily in the form of concepts but in accounts of following Christ."[31] Metz is correct. Human lives, or "life stories," can indeed serve as a source for theology, as numerous theologians have displayed in recent years.[32] More specifically, we can learn about Jesus Christ by looking at the lives of his disciples, some of whom are our contemporaries. This means, quite concretely, that using autobiographies and biographies as theological sources can contribute both to our understanding of God and to our grasp of the concepts used in religious discourse.

While Kasper has not explicitly discussed the role of exemplary Christian lives in theology, his comments on Christology point toward this in two ways. First, the starting place for our elucidation of the confession that Jesus is the Christ is the Church's current experience of the risen Christ. It begins with the kerygma as heard today. Thus he writes:

> We should not remove the Jesus tradition from the context of proclamation, liturgy and parish practice of the Christian churches. Only where the message of Jesus Christ is alive and believed, where that same Spirit is alive who enlivens the writings of the New Testament, can the testimony of the New Testament be understood as a living witness.[33]

Kasper's insistence that Christology springs from communities where "the message of Jesus Christ is alive and believed" prompts us to pay attention to Christian lives. The New Testament's proclamation can be grasped as "a living witness" where it is in fact embodied by specific women and men. Systematic inquiry makes little sense without such a background, for as he states: "Even today, therefore, the community of the Church is the proper location of the Jesus tradition and encounter with Christ."[34]

Second, this starting point is indirectly expressed in Kasper's work when he includes contemporary life and thought as a theological source along with Scripture and tradition and history.[35] In *Jesus the Christ* this source is the post-Enlightenment idea of freedom. As we saw in Chapter Two, Kasper brings the notion of liberation to his interpretation of historical data and tradition. Kasper's reliance on this third source confirms the importance of Christian lives, for it is women and men who have critically appropriated contemporary thought and experience in light of the Christian heritage. For example, the idea of freedom presented by Kasper was in fact embodied by Dorothy Day in her commitment to nurture a new form of life in American society. Thus, even though Kasper does not explicitly discuss the role of biography in Christology, his method implicitly supports this.

Such an approach therefore indicates the appropriateness of referring to Christian biographies in doing Christology, but we need to look more closely at *how* such life stories can contribute to our attempts to identify Jesus Christ. We can do this by extending Ricoeur's discussion of a narrative's sense and its reference to the use of biographies in theology.

A biography's sense, we saw, stems from its narrative structure. The recollection of a life is a form of history. Moreover, this personal history is characterized by reliance on those metaphors that have influenced the actual life. All of us—consciously or unconsciously—live by a set of images and stories. Terence Tilley gives the example of the saints: "The martyrs picked out from Christ's life key motifs—metaphors—that they could use to structure their own life and adapt his story for their own."[36] A person's identity is therefore linked to specific figurations, and a Christian's identity is determined by Scripture's and tradition's images and stories about Christ.

The lives of exemplary Christians manifest the deliberate appropriation of motifs taken from the Scriptures, especially from the Gospels. In Tilley's words: "To be a disciple of Christ is to be a member of his body, to take the stories of the Christian tradition and to adapt or adopt them to be one's own story."[37] Dorothy Day, for instance, chose to shape her life according to the parable of the sheep and goats (Mt 25:31–46), taking literally the injunction to feed the hungry, clothe the naked, and house the homeless. Or, to take other examples cited by William McClendon, Dag Hammarskjold adopted the Gospel image of servant, while Martin Luther King, Jr. deliberately lived by the motif of the exodus and the promised land. McClendon writes:

> [A] key to these biographies is the dominant or controlling *images* which may be found in the lives of which they speak. Dag Hammarskjold and Martin Luther King, Jr., it can be shown, were each possessed of certain characteristic images . . . by which each understood himself, faced the critical situations in his life, and chiseled out his own destiny. I take it that the convergence of such images in a particular person helps to form his characteristic vision or outlook.[38]

Biographies can contribute to Christology by disclosing the images of Christ by which exemplary Christians have lived. In other words, biography's role here depends at least in part upon its sense. The governing metaphors of a life can align with the motifs generated by the Gospels and by historical research about Jesus to create a single representation of the risen Christ. But something more must be noted. The use of life story in Christology is also a function of a biography's reference.

A biography makes sense on its own terms. It does not receive its meaning by being linked with the actual person about whom it is written. Rather, in part, a biography means what it says. As we saw in Chapter One, a biography identifies a person not so much by pointing to him or her—as a name does—as by describing the person. Such an account has a coherence that allows it to stand on its own, as a narrative in its own right. Yet, since a biography does refer to a life, it needs to be measured against this actual life, this enacted narrative. To some extent, therefore, a biography refers as all forms of history do. It gathers reports and testimonies that point to the life. Thus a biography simultaneously stands on its own and also refers to its actual subject. But can a biography also refer to Jesus Christ?

While a biography refers primarily to its subject, that is, to the man or woman whose life is recounted, it can secondarily refer to another person—the person who served as the subject's role model. It can therefore shed light on this second person as known through the eyes of the primary subject. In the life stories of exemplary Christians, this secondary reference occurs because the subject has taken his or her bearings from Christ, as manifest in tradition and in the Church. For instance, after her conversion, Dorothy Day sought to live in response to the Lord whom she met in the celebration of sacraments, personal prayer and service of neighbor. What occurred in Day's life is also found in other Christian lives. A Christian's life points beyond itself to the risen Lord. As Clebsch writes: "[I]t is true that the figure who furnished the history of Christianity with its fundamental continuity has been Jesus Christ. Always and everywhere Christians have made him the model for their religiousness."[39] In light of Clebsch's point, an accurate recounting of a Christian life refers primarily to its subject, but it also refers secondarily to Jesus Christ.

A Christian biography can manifest Christ's presence in contemporary affairs. Its sense and reference make known not only the identity of the biography's subject, but also the person of the risen Lord. The history of an exemplary Christian recollects the life of a specific woman or man, and yet it also expresses the enacted narrative of Christ abiding with the human community, thereby picking up where the Gospels leave off. "If the church is the body of Christ," writes Tilley, "its members continue the work of Christ in the world. To continue to tell the story of Christ is to tell the stories of the members of his body."[40] Conversely, to recount the lives of the saints is to tell the story of Christ today.

Christian biographies are *one* source for Christology, but they are not the sole source. They do not stand alone, for they function in Christology along with historical narratives and the Gospels. These three different kinds of narratives can contribute to an inquiry because each provides a distinct perspective on the same subject: Jesus Christ. Moreover, these narratives do not represent the totality of Christology's three sources. Tradition, for instance, also includes the Church's doctrinal formulations. Yet, narratives do relate Scripture and tradition, historical study, and the contemporary Church in such a way that together they convey the person, Jesus Christ, who, alive in the Spirit, abides in history.

To this point, we have clarified two claims that undergird the use of narratives in a Christology of reciprocity. First, just as other human lives can be envisaged as enacted narratives, so too can Christ's life. The context of Jesus' words and deeds, especially of his passion and death, is a "history" that extends beyond his crucifixion to his second coming. Second, more than one kind of narrative is required to express this enacted narrative, Jesus Christ. Historical narrative, the Gospels and Christian biography manifest this person who already participates in God's new creation. Following upon these two claims, we can now consider our third and final claim.

III. *Narratives and Systematic Inquiry*

Knowledge of a person entails more than knowing the person's biography. As was noted in Chapter One, the question "Who is so-and-so?" leads not only to the recollection of a life but also to reflection upon this life. It can prompt us, for instance, to ask how this person (e.g., Dorothy Day or Dag Hammarskjold) confronts and resolves the basic issues of human life and also how this life stands in relation to God. These kinds of questions require answers which are straightforwardly stated not in narrative but in conceptual discourse. The issue of personal identity directs an investigation beyond figurative terms to more notional ones, for example, beyond the image of Jesus Christ as founder to the idea of Jesus Christ as self-agent. Or, to cite another instance, to resolve issues concerning the person of Jesus Christ, the Council of Chalcedon shifted from biblical imagery to the language of *ousia* ("being") and *hypostasis* ("person"). This recognition of Christology's reliance on both figurative speech and discursive language brings us to a discussion of our third conviction: the explicit use of narratives in Christology serves to specify the notions of person operative in systematic inquiry.

The relationship of narrative to discursive speech in theology is currently receiving scholarly attention. Metz has noted, for example, that theology's argumentation is derived from narrative. He writes: "The verbal content of Christianity should therefore be seen primarily as a major narrative which contains argumentative structures and elements and produces such structures."[41] A similar insight has been fruitfully pursued by other theologians and philosophers, but rather than reviewing their views, I would like here simply to clarify one aspect of narratives' role in theological argument by highlighting aspects of what we have already seen in previous chapters.[42]

In *Jesus* Schillebeeckx has shown that an historical narrative about Jesus can generate a new Christology. It can do so because the gathering of historical data about Jesus affords an insight into his identity, and this insight can in turn produce fresh concepts about Jesus. A process like this occurred, Schillebeeckx contends, among Jesus' first followers. Impressions of Jesus circulated among his disciples, and as they coalesced they resulted in a fresh disclosure of Jesus' identity. This discovery took the form of seeing and proclaiming Jesus as the eschatological prophet.

What took place among the first Christians, says Schillebeeckx, can be repeated over and over again. The theologian can recall some of the details of Jesus' ministry, thereby producing an historical narrative which in turn leads to an insight expressed in conceptual terms. As Schillebeeckx states: "[A] real source experience (one that sees an unfathomable depth disclosed in historically observable data) in being experienced evokes for itself models of its own."[43] In other words, an historical narrative about Jesus can give rise to models or concepts needed for systematic reflection on the person and work of Jesus Christ.

Schillebeeckx's position is amplified in general terms by Ricoeur who, in numerous writings, has investigated the relationship between narrative and theory.[44] Simply on the basis of Ricoeur's essay "The Narrative Function" this much can be said: Plot, a constitutive element in narrative, consists of both an "episodic dimension" and a "configurational element." The latter conveys in images the unity of discrete elements, and these images are the point of departure for theoretical accounts of this unity. For example, the recounting of a history includes both episodic and configurational dimensions, the latter giving the basis for an historian's explanation of this history. In Ricoeur's words: "[T]he explanatory procedures of scientific history cannot replace a prior narrative but function in conjunction with it, insofar as they are grafted onto its configurational structure."[45] This point can be extended to theology: systematic inquiry about Jesus Christ does not replace narratives about him, but draws upon the images and ideas produced by these narratives.

Schillebeeckx's and Ricoeur's reflections on figuration and theory are insightful. They reveal that the relation of narrative to discursive speech is not one of opposition, but of continuity. Narrative is source for the models upon which theory depends. According to MacIntyre "the concept of a person is that of a character abstracted from a history."[46] A recollection of what someone said and did is the ground from which concepts of that person emerge, and when these ideas are uprooted from this ground, they lose their meaning. In other words, the notions used in Christology to speak of the personhood of Christ gain their specificity from the narratives with which they are associated. This assessment is confirmed by what we have seen in van Beeck's *Christ Proclaimed*, in Chapter Five's Christological exercise, and in Kasper's *Jesus the Christ*.

Van Beeck's recollection of the Synoptic story shows Jesus reaching out to others, even when he is rejected by them—a pattern that culminates with his crucifixion. This narrative raises then a question about the source of Jesus' persistence. What enabled Jesus to live and die as "the man for others"?[47] The answer relies on the idea of person as relation, and yet this conceptual language is simultaneously defined by the story that prompted the question.

In general, talk about the relating of "I"-"Thou" can have a range of meanings, expressed for example in such expressions as "individual self-realization," "mutual giving and receiving," and "self-sacrifice." The story of Jesus' outreach to others, despite their misunderstanding and rejection of him, specifies a self-sacrificial sense of "I"-"Thou." Jesus bears the "good news" to others without demanding their positive response to him. His care is unilateral. Moreover, Jesus' relating springs from his bond with God: Jesus persists in his mission because of his intimacy with Abba. These aspects of the Synoptic story define person as relation, when the relating is characterized by that in the sense of the self-sacrificial concern for others that originates from a theocentric point of reference. If *Christ Proclaimed* did not briefly recount the story of Matthew, Mark and Luke, its last chapters would be ambiguous. Here is an instance in which a narrative has specified the meaning of conceptual discourse.

This same linking of narrative and theory occurs in my reflection on Jesus Christ as God's agent (Chapter Five). An historical narrative about Jesus, the retelling of Mark's Gospel, and a biography of Dorothy Day converge to yield the image of Jesus Christ as the founder of the new people of compassion. This image, in turn, focuses the language of self-agency. Jesus is an individual who enacts his intentions, initiates change, and assumes responsibility for his actions. More precisely, in light of the three narratives and the image of founder, we can say that Jesus fulfills God's intention to be united with creation, and he simultaneously realizes humankind's aspiration to be reconciled with God. Jesus Christ integrates therefore both divine and human intentions, and this insight provides content for the statement that Jesus Christ is God's agent.

Finally, *Jesus the Christ* illumines the relation of narrative to discursive speech because of what it does and does not do. Kasper's work displays in detail the historical development of concepts of Jesus Christ. For example, the presentations on the Son of God, the Son of man, and the mediator treat biblical testimony, patristic teaching, medieval writings, Reformation and Counter-Reformation thought, Enlightenment views, and post-Enlightenment ideas. This balanced analysis shows how primitive insights into God's selflessness and Jesus' identity, as expressed in the Bible, have been refined and deepened in more theoretical terms. Scriptural figuration has generated centuries of notional clarifications about God and Jesus. Kasper's discussions would be even stronger, however, if they included explicit recollections of the biblical motifs that nurtured later conceptual accounts of Jesus' person and work. The intelligibility of these ideas suffers when they are treated in abtraction from such foundational narrative motifs as Philippians 2, Romans 8, and 1 Timothy 3.

Kasper himself has stressed the importance of keeping narrative and theory together. In his words: "[W]e cannot pit a narrative Christology against an argumentative Christology."[48] Both are vital to systematic inquiry. Further, he has reiterated this point in relation to the doctrine of Chalcedon, which, in his judgment, "represents a contradiction." The Chalcedonean decree abstracts the issue of Jesus' "nature" and "person" from the context of his life, yet to be properly understood it needs to be seen in relation to the Bible. Kasper states: "Even though the Christological dogma of Chalcedon is a permanently binding interpretation of Scripture, it nevertheless has to be integrated into the total biblical testimony and interpreted in its light."[49] Kasper's perception is corroborated by Brian McDermott, who writes:

> *Ousia* and *hypostasis* language is the perfectly valid if limited way of summarizing Jesus' history with his Father and us in the unifying and freeing power of the Spirit. Without the telling of the story ever anew [however], the metaphysics of *ousia* and *hypostasis* loses its life and becomes blockage for believers.[50]

Narrative's relation to conceptual discourse is therefore one not of opposition, but of continuity. Moreover, as our analyses have demonstrated, narrative gives the precise meaning of the notions of person employed in Christology. The retelling of the Synoptic story, or the recounting of an historical narrative, in conjunction with the Gospels and with the study of Christian biography, is not the last word but yields to conceptual discourse. Recollections such as these, conversely, determine systematic inquiry's use of such notions as person as relation and person as self-agent. Our third claim can then be reiterated by stating that in Christology narratives can give specificity to conceptual discourse.

IV. *Christology Shaped by Story*

Three claims have received our attention. First, a human life can be envisaged as an enacted narrative, and so too can Christ's life, though it breaks our accustomed temporal and spatial frameworks. Second, history and fiction provide distinct, though complementary perspectives on personal existence. Similarly, historical narrative, Gospel and Christian biography can afford separate, yet mutually enriching accounts of Jesus Christ. Third, rather than standing in opposition to theory, narration contributes to it by specifying how notional terms function. These three points shed light therefore on the rationale for using different kinds of narrative within a Christology of reciprocity. With these clarifications, let us conclude by recalling our proposal.

One urgent issue facing the Church today concerns the identity of Jesus Christ, as is evident in a variety of recent official statements. At the start of their respective pontificates both Paul VI and John Paul II stressed the centrality of Jesus Christ to the Church's renewal.[51] Further, in 1980 the International Theological Commission focused on emerging topics in Christology with its publication of *Select Questions on Christology,* and in 1985 the Pontifical Biblical Commission clarified the relation of Scripture to inquiry about Jesus Christ in its report *Bible and Christology.*[52] Church authorities are clearly aware of Christology's importance today.

The need for a renewal of Christology has also been urged by a number of astute observers of Christian life. Robert Imbelli of Boston College, for instance, has observed: "Every genuine renewal of the church has been animated by a new realization of the presence and power of Christ—whether by Benedict or Francis, Ignatius or Teresa, Vincent de Paul or Charles de Foucauld."[53] Therefore, says Imbelli, one of theology's current tasks is that of promoting a "new Christ-mysticism"— a task to be undertaken by uniting theology and spirituality. Parallel to Imbelli's appraisal is that of John Catoir, director of The Christophers, who writes: "My own instinct is that the Catholic Church has not emphasized Jesus Christ enough in its teaching. He is certainly central to the Church, but the popular perception of Catholicism is that it is more issue-oriented than Christ-centered."[54] These are but two voices among others. The Christian assembly is currently seeking a fuller understanding of Jesus Christ.

In *Jesus the Christ* Kasper has inquired into the identity of Jesus using a Christology of reciprocity. This method's focal question is "Who is Jesus Christ today?" And the three sources for answering this are Scripture and tradition, history, and the Church's recent experience and thought. This third source, contemporary faith, is at least partially recognized by Kasper in the role he gives to the post-Enlightenment view of freedom, an aspiration that can be realized, he argues, only with assistance from outside the human condition. This accent of freedom serves as Kasper's point of view for both his historical study of Jesus' ministry and his analysis of Scripture and tradition. As a result, Jesus Christ is identified as the mediator between God and creation. He lived and died in fidelity to God, and therefore with his resurrection he has released the Spirit of freedom within history. He has set all people free to live for God and neighbor, because he has himself already lived this way.

A Christology of reciprocity provides an accurate and balanced response to today's interest in Jesus Christ. However, in Chapter Five we saw how its threefold method can be strengthened through the explicit use of different kinds of narratives about Jesus. Just as our ordinary attempts to say who someone is depend upon knowledge of a biographical kind, so too our efforts to identify Jesus Christ can benefit by our recounting various narratives about Jesus. Theologically speaking, an historical narrative alone is not sufficient for the task, so that other forms of narrative are also required. These are the Gospels as stories and instances of Christian biography. These three kinds of narrative are properly situated within what Kasper has singled out as Christology's three sources: Scripture and tradition, history, and the contemporary Church's life and thought.

This explicit use of narratives in systematic inquiry about Jesus could be called "story-shaped Christology." Whereas the expression "narrative Christology" could be construed to mean the reduction of theology to storytelling, "Christology shaped by story" means that narratives function within a larger, intellectually-disciplined, investigation. Further, "story" in the strict sense is the category to which the Gospels belong, and the Gospels play a primary role in this Christology. They directly contribute as one of three narrative sources. Moreover, they indirectly influence this theological reflection in that exemplary Christians like Dorothy Day have based their lives on the Gospels, so that to recall the life of a saint is to observe how one person enacted the Gospels. In sum, the Gospels' direct and indirect contribution under the terms of a reciprocal method results in what can be accurately described as "story-shaped Christology."

"And to make an end," says T. S. Eliot in *Little Gidding,* "is to make a beginning." Such is definitely the case in Christology. At the outset of *Jesus the Christ,* Kasper writes: "Jesus Christ is one of those figures with whom you are never finished once you have begun to explore his personality."[55] Reflection on Jesus Christ engenders further inquiry into this person and what he has brought about. As I conclude this study, I have to admit that this will not be the last word about Jesus Christ. A more complete story-shaped Christology would draw not only on narratives but also on other elements within each of the three sources (e.g., patristic writings and the Christological councils).

There is another sense, too, in which a Christology is not an end but a beginning. Study of Jesus Christ leads beyond itself to inquiry into the reality of God. As we gain insight into the person and work of Jesus Christ, we encounter issues about Jesus' relation with God and hence about the character of God. To put this another way, once we recall biblical stories about Jesus, for example, the Gospels or the kenosis hymn (Phil 2:6–11), we realize that these must be set within a yet larger narrative, the story of God.[56] Christology brings us to the threshold of reflection on the triune God.

As Kasper has rightly acknowledged, we are never finished in our pursuit of Christ's identity. Once we set out to know this person in a systematic inquiry, we discover the overwhelming wealth of his words, deeds and persistent presence in history. Our study has clarified the importance of different kinds of narratives for this quest. The effort to identify Jesus Christ is best realized when we explicitly employ the Gospels as stories, historical narratives about Jesus, and biographies of exemplary Christians within Christology.

NOTES

1. William Clebsch, *Christianity in European History* (New York: Oxford University Press, 1979), p. 12. Cf. Jaroslav Pelikan, *Jesus Through the Centuries* (New Haven: Yale University Press, 1985).

2. Cf. Anthony E. Harvey, "Christian Propositions and Christian Stories," in: *idem* (ed.), *God Incarnate* (London: SPCK, 1981), pp. 1–13; Stephen Sykes, "The Incarnation as the Foundation of the Church," in: A. E. Harvey (ed.), *God Incarnate,* pp. 115–127; John Navone and Thomas Cooper, *Tellers of the Word* (New York: Le Jacq Publishing, 1981); Josef Meyer zu Schlochtern, "Erzählung als paradigma einer alternativen theologischen Denkform," in: J. Pfammatter and F. Furger (eds.), *Theologische Berichte 8* (Zurich: Benziger Verlag, 1979), pp. 35–70; *idem, Glaube—Sprache—Erfahrung* (Bern: Verlag Peter Lang, 1978).

3. Johannes B. Metz, "An Identity Crisis in Christianity: Transcendental and Political Responses," in: William J. Kelly (ed.), *Theology and Discovery* (Milwaukee: Marquette University Press, 1980), pp. 169–178, 171.

4. Alasdair MacIntyre, *After Virtue* (Notre Dame: University of Notre Dame Press, 1981), pp. 190–203.

5. Paul Ricoeur, "The Narrative Function," in: P. Ricoeur, *Hermeneutics and the Human Sciences,* edited by John B. Thompson (Cambridge: Cambridge University Press, 1981), pp. 274–296.

6. This chapter provides therefore not so much a foundational theology as a descriptive theology. Cf. Ronald F. Thiemann, *Revelation and Theology* (Notre Dame: University of Notre Dame Press, 1985); George Lindbeck, *The Nature of Doctrine* (Philadelphia: The Westminster Press, 1984); articles by James Buckley, Coleman O'Neill, William Placher, and David Tracy, in *The Thomist,* XL (1985).

7. Stephen Crites, "The Narrative Quality of Experience," *Journal of the American Academy of Religion,* XXXIX (1971), 291–311; Barbara Hardy, *Tellers and Listeners* (London: The Atlone Press, 1975); cf. Patricia Wismer, "The Myth of Original Sin" (University of Chicago: Ph.D. dissertation, 1983), pp. 94–98.

8. MacIntyre, *After Virtue,* p. 191.

9. *Ibid.,* p. 194.

10. *Ibid.,* p. 197.

11. *Ibid.,* p. 202.

12. *Ibid.,* p. 203.

13. Johann B. Metz, *Faith in History and Society,* trans. D. Smith (New York: Seabury Press, 1980), p. 212.

14. Walter Kasper, *Jesus the Christ,* trans. V. Green (New York: Paulist Press, 1976), pp. 168, 172.

15. Cf. Thomas F. Tracy, *God, Action and Embodiment* (Grand Rapids: William B. Eerdmanns, 1984); Eberhard Jüngel, *God as the Mystery of the World,* trans. D. L. Guder (Grand Rapids: William B. Eerdmans, 1983), pp. 343–367.

16. Brother Roger Schutz, "Interview," *America,* CLII (January 22, 1983), p. 50.

17. Ricoeur, "The Narrative Function," p. 294. On Ricoeur's view of narrative in comparison with Hans Frei's, see: Gary Comstock, "Truth or Meaning: Ricoeur versus Frei on Biblical Narrative," *Journal of Religion,* LXVI (April 1986), 117–140.

18. Robert Scholes and Robert Kellogg, *The Nature of Narrative* (New York: Oxford University Press, 1966), p. 207.

19. Ricoeur, "The Narrative Function," pp. 279.

20. *Ibid.,* p. 284.

21. *Ibid.,* pp. 287–288.

22. *Ibid.,* p. 293.

23. *Ibid.,* pp. 296.

24. Cf. Paul Ricoeur, *Time and Narrative,* Vols. I and II, trans. K. McLaughlin and D. Pellauer (Chicago: University of Chicago Press, 1984).

25. Cf. Paul Ricoeur, "Toward a Hermeneutic of the Idea of Revelation," *Harvard Theological Review,* LXX (January–April, 1977); *idem,* "From Proclamation to Narrative," *Journal of Religion,* LXIV (1984), 501–512.

26. William Poteat, "Myths, Stories, History, Eschatology and Action: Some Polanyian Meditations," in: Thomas Langford and W. Poteat (eds.), *Intellect and Hope* (Durham: Duke University Press, 1968), pp. 198–231, 226.

27. Edward Schillebeeckx, *Jesus,* trans. H. Hoskins (New York: Seabury Press, 1979), pp. 77–80, 77.

28. This is not to deny that the Gospels belong to their own literary genre. Cf. Norman Perrin and Dennis C. Duling, *The New Testament,* second edition (San Diego: Harcourt Brace Jovanovich Publishers, 1982), pp. 40, 76.

29. Hans W. Frei, *The Identity of Jesus Christ* (Philadelphia: Fortress Press, 1975), p. xiv.

30. Ricoeur, "The Narrative Function," p. 290.

31. Johann B. Metz, *Followers of Christ,* trans. T. Linton (New York: Paulist Press, 1978), p. 40.

32. James Wm. McClendon, Jr., *Ethics: Systematic Theology,* Vol. I (Nashville: Abingdon, 1986); *idem, Biography as Theology* (Nashville: Abingdon Press, 1974); Terrence W. Tilley, *Story Theology* (Wilmington: Michael Glazier, 1985), pp. 147–181; Brian McDermott, "The Christ-Wound: Christology and Teresa of Avila," *Word and Spirit,* IV (1983), 32–53. Cf. *idem,* "Jesus Christ in Today's Faith and Theology," in: Edward Schillebeeckx and Johannes B. Metz (eds.), *Jesus, Son of God?* (New York: The Seabury Press, 1982), pp. 3–10; Stanley Hauerwas, *Truthfulness and Tragedy* (Notre Dame: University of Notre Dame Press, 1977), pp. 82–100; Sally McFague [TeSelle], *Speaking in Parables* (Philadelphia: Fortress Press, 1975), pp. 145–180; David

Burrell, *Exercises in Religious Understanding* (Notre Dame: University of Notre Dame Press, 1974), pp. 9–42.

33. Kasper, *Jesus the Christ*, p. 27.

34. *Ibid.*

35. *Ibid*, pp. 52–58.

36. Tilley, *Story Theology*, p. 153.

37. *Ibid.*, p. 176.

38. McClendon, *Biography as Theology*, pp. 89–90.

39. Clebsch, *Christianity in European History*, p. 13.

40. Tilley, *Story Theology*, p. 147.

41. Metz, *Faith in History and Society*, p. 216.

42. Cf. Eberhard Jüngel, *God as the Mystery of the World*, pp. 299–314; *idem, Entsprechungen: Gott—Wahrheit—Mensch* (Munich: Chr. Kaiser, 1986), pp. 103–157; Stanley Hauerwas, *The Peaceable Kingdom* (Notre Dame: University of Notre Dame Press, 1983); David Burrell, "Argument in Theology: Analogy and Narrative," in: Carl Raschke (ed.), *New Dimensions in Philosophical Theology* (Chico: Scholars Press, 1982), pp. 37–51; George Stroup, *The Promise of Narrative Theology* (Atlanta: John Knox Press, 1981).

43. Schillebeeckx, *Jesus*, p. 571; *idem, Interim Report*, pp. 10–19, 32.

44. Paul Ricoeur, "The Bible and the Imagination," in: Hans Dieter Betz (ed.), *The Bible as a Document of the University* (Chico: Scholars Press, 1981); *idem, Interpretation Theory* (Fort Worth: Texas University Press, 1976); *idem*, "The Specificity of Religious Language," in: John Dominic Crossan (ed.), *Semeia #4* (Missoula: Scholars Press, 1975), pp. 107–148.

45. Ricoeur, "The Narrative Function," p. 280.

46. MacIntyre, *After Virtue*, p. 202.

47. Frans Jozef van Beeck, *Christ Proclaimed* (New York: Paulist Press, 1979), p. 375.

48. Kasper, *Jesus the Christ*, p. 20.

49. *Ibid.*, p. 238.

50. Brian McDermott, "Roman Catholic Christology," *Theological Studies*, XLI (1980), pp. 339–367, 359.

51. Paul VI, "The Opening Address at the Second Session of the Second Vatican Council" (September 29, 1963), in: Xavier Rynne, *The Second Session* (New York: Farrar, Straus and Company, 1963), pp. 347–363; John Paul II, *The Redeemer of Man* (Washington, D.C.: United States Catholic Conference, 1983).

52. International Theological Commission, *Select Questions on Christology* (Washington, D.C.: United States Catholic Conference, 1980); Joseph Fitzmyer, *Scripture and Christology* (New York: Paulist Press, 1986).

53. Robert Imbelli, "The Return of 'Mystery'," *Commonweal*, CXIII

(January 31, 1986), 41–44, 43. Recent works that unite theology and spirituality include: Kenneth Leech, *Experiencing God* (San Francisco: Harper and Row, 1985); Rowan Williams, *Resurrection* (London: Darton, Longman and Todd, 1982).

54. John Catoir, "Fundamentalists on the Move," *America,* CLV (September 27, 1986), 142–144, 143.

55. Kasper, *Jesus the Christ,* p. 41.

56. Cf. Catherine Mowry LaCugna, "Re-Conceiving the Trinity as the Mystery of Salvation," *The Scottish Journal of Theology,* XXXVIII (1986), 1–23; Walter Kasper, *The God of Jesus Christ,* trans. M. J. O'Connell (New York: Crossroad, 1984); Eberhard Jüngel, *God as the Mystery of the World,* pp. 343–396.

THEOLOGICAL INQUIRIES:

Serious studies on contemporary questions of Scripture, Systematics and Moral Theology. Also in the series: